# MEANIN

## The F

Jen Shang and Adrian Sargeant

With a Foreword by
Tony Bury

P

First published in Great Britain in 2024 by

Policy Press, an imprint of
Bristol University Press
University of Bristol
1–9 Old Park Hill
Bristol
BS2 8BB
UK
t: +44 (0)117 374 6645
e: bup-info@bristol.ac.uk

Details of international sales and distribution partners are available at
policy.bristoluniversitypress.co.uk

British Library Cataloguing in Publication Data
A catalogue record for this book is available from the British Library

ISBN 978-1-4473-7176-2 paperback
ISBN 978-1-4473-7177-9 ePub
ISBN 978-1-4473-7178-6 ePdf

Cover design: Robin Hawes
Front cover image: istock/SvetaZi

# Contents

# List of figures and tables

## Figures

## Tables

# About the authors

**Jen Shang,** Professor of Philanthropic Psychology, is Co-Founder and Co-Director of the Institute for Sustainable Philanthropy. She is the world's first PhD in Philanthropy and the world's only philanthropic psychologist. Her research has been covered in *The New York Times, The Guardian, The Chronicle of Philanthropy, Advancing Philanthropy* and *The Nonprofit Times,* and by the BBC. Jen has been published in numerous academic journals, including the *Journal of Marketing Research, Marketing Science, The Economic Journal, Experimental Economics, Organizational Behavior and Human Decision Processes,* the *Nonprofit and Voluntary Sector Quarterly* and *Nonprofit Management and Leadership.* Her research has been funded by the Society for Judgment and Decision Making, the National Science Foundation, the Aspen Institute, the Corporation for Public Broadcasting, the Association of Fundraising Professionals and the Hewlett Foundation.

**Adrian Sargeant** is Co-Founder and Co-Director of the Institute for Sustainable Philanthropy. He was formerly the first Hartsook Chair in Fundraising at the Lilly Family School of Philanthropy at Indiana University. Adrian is a Visiting Professor of Fundraising at Avila University and at the Australian Centre for Philanthropy and Nonprofit Studies, Queensland University of Technology. In 2010 he was included in *The Nonprofit Times'* prestigious Power and Influence list in the US, and in the same year he received a Civil Society award in the UK for his services to the profession of fundraising. In 2016 he received a lifetime achievement award from the Institute of Fundraising (now the Chartered Institute of Fundraising). Adrian designed the UK's system of professional education for fundraisers and has recently redesigned the European qualification framework for the European Fundraising Association. Adrian is listed by Research. com as one of the UK's leading business and management academics, having published 249 articles and been cited over 8,000 times by his peers.

# Acknowledgements

The authors gratefully acknowledge the kindness and generosity of Anne and Tony Bury, without whom this research would not have been possible.

# Foreword

*Tony Bury*
*Formerly a leading business*
*developer in the Middle East and Chair of 3sixty*
*Capital. Founder of The Human Edge*
*(previously known as Mowgli Mentoring) and a*
*catalytic philanthropist*

Some people are incurable romantics or artists. I have always been an incurable learner, a seeker. Though I enjoyed a less-than-average early academic life, this changed when I was given the gift of 'the power of learning' while spending an extensive period in hospital prior to sitting my O levels. So, call me an incurable learner. This led to success at A levels, university and then an MBA. In my first years in the workplace, working within two large corporates, I recognised that that was not for me. I needed to nourish my insatiable appetite for learning and experiencing with what Malcolm Gladwell aptly describes as 'meaningful work'. For me, this encompassed working with autonomy, using my brain and seeing a direct relationship between effort and reward.

This propelled me on to an entrepreneurial journey during which I established a considerable number of startups – some successful, some not so successful and others failures. Each of them fed my craving for curiosity, learning and development. My great mentor John O'Neil (author of *The Paradox of Success*) identified early on in our relationship that I had lived a life of jumping from one learning curve to the next. My next jump led me to philanthropy, founding and operating Mowgli Mentoring, now rebranded as The Human Edge (https://humanedge.org.uk/). On handing over Mowgli, after ten years leading the organisation, to my daughter Kat, she commenced her own learning curve. I had become a seeker of wisdom, meaning; that was my true calling. Laterally, I have extended my philanthropy into a combination of regular 'community' giving and 'catalytic' philanthropic opportunities.

While my 'giving' began in my early twenties, my real focus on philanthropy commenced just over 15 years ago. During this period, I have had the pleasure of meeting many high-net-worth individuals (HNWIs) and ultra-high-net-worth individuals (UHNWIs) – some have undertaken philanthropy, though I perceive that the majority have not. I became increasingly curious to learn what the catalyst could be for someone to become a philanthropist and, likewise, why some may not go down this path. What is that magical trigger, ignition and fusion, if you like? Upon further reflection, my search added the following four questions, which have anchored themselves, over all these years, in both my head and my heart:

- What are the barriers people experience in their philanthropy and how do they overcome them?
- What determines their focus in their philanthropy?
- How do they experience their philanthropy?
- Can the results help both philanthropists and fundraisers to meet their objectives?

These questions shaped the research for the book that you have in your hands and are reading today.

In seeking the right person to undertake this research, I was very fortunate to be introduced to Professor Jen Shang at the Institute for Sustainable Philanthropy. Jen, a philanthropic psychologist, was the first person to be awarded a PhD in Philanthropy. She was the ideal person to conduct the research. Unburdened, unbiased, uncluttered and unrelenting expertise such as hers is hard to come by these days.

This is the beginning, and I am curious where it will lead us. I would very much welcome cooperation and collaboration with fellow philanthropists and philanthropic organisations on this journey, and not least with those HNWIs, UHNWIs and entrepreneurs who are considering embarking on their own philanthropic journeys. Our ultimate goal is to increase 'giving' while making the experience more meaningful for philanthropists. Should you have any thoughts, contributions or wish to join us on this journey, please contact Jen Shang (Jen@philanthropy-institute.org.uk).

I would like to thank Jen and her team as well as all the interviewees who gave their time and insights so willingly and so meaningfully. As Rumi says so eloquently: 'I am yours. Don't give myself back to me.'

# 1

# Introduction

This is a book about the experience of philanthropy. A plethora of texts have explored the search for philanthropic impact and the difference that wealthy philanthropists can make in their focal communities. How to create and maximise that impact is an obvious and important subject for study. Yet there has been little interest in how that philanthropy is experienced by such donors and the psychological benefits it can potentially deliver, including the provision of a deep sense of personal meaning and purpose in life. It turns out that these benefits are hugely important for philanthropists' sense of self, but also for their focal communities, because enhanced meaning also makes philanthropy more sustainable, even in the face of what can appear quite insurmountable challenges.

The research on which this book is based is the first to examine the major challenges that high-net-worth individuals (HNWIs) and ultra-high-net-worth individuals (UHNWIs) must overcome in order to create the most meaningful philanthropy. To the best of our knowledge, it is the first time that theories of meaning and meaningfulness have been applied to the philanthropic domain and to the study of HNWIs in particular.

UHNWIs are commonly understood to be those with liquid assets of $30 million and over, while HNWIs are viewed as people who own liquid assets valued from $1 million up to $30 million. The thresholds typically include liquid assets only (money held in bank or brokerage accounts) and exclude assets, such as the value of a primary residence. In 2020, 11.6 million American households held a net worth of $1 million to $5 million, excluding the value of their primary residence (Spectrum Group, 2021). The top ten countries by HNWI population in 2021 were the US, Japan, Germany, China, France, the UK, Switzerland, Canada, Italy and the Netherlands (Capgemini, 2021).

Unsurprisingly, there has been a great deal of academic and professional interest in the behaviour of high-net-worth groups. A large amount of literature examines the relationship between income, net wealth and charitable giving (for example, Wiepking and Bekkers, 2012; Meer and Priday, 2021; Neumayr and Pennerstorfer, 2021). Studies have also examined the demographic characteristics of givers (for example, Prince and File, 1994; Hickman et al, 2015; Coupe and Monteiro, 2016), how they give (for example, MacAskill, 2016; Osili et al, 2019; Duquette and Hargaden, 2021; Sellen, 2021), what entities they give to (for example, Coutts, 2017; Osili et al, 2021), how well they give (for example, Dalzell, 2013; Eikenberry and Mirabella, 2018; Buchanan, 2019; Collins and Flannery, 2020; Davids and Meijs, 2020; Reich, 2020; Brooks and Kumar, 2021) and why they give (for example, Nielsen, 1985; Boris, 1987; Dunlop, 1993; Ostrower, 1995; Schervish et al, 2001; Frumkin, 2006; Havens et al, 2006; Osili, 2011; Breeze and Lloyd, 2013; Herzog and Price, 2016). A detailed review of this scholarly literature is beyond the scope of this text, but a brief explanation of the key motives of HNWIs and UHNWIs is warranted to set our study in its proper context.

Motives for philanthropy are often depicted as a dichotomy of altruism versus self-interest, or perhaps a hybrid of the two. Altruism is typically defined as giving driven exclusively by a concern with the benefits provided to others. It often reflects an obligation on the part of the wealthy to 'do the right thing' or act in accordance with their moral principles, values or religious faith. It can also, of course, reflect a genuine identification with the needs of others (Bekkers and Wiepking, 2011). This stands in contrast to self-interested giving, in which givers receive something in return for a gift – for example, enhanced reputation, recognition, social status, important relationships, tax benefits or the ability to limit the scale of the inheritance available to their heirs (Bekkers and Wiepking, 2011; Worth et al, 2019). In the case of the latter, many UHNWIs speak of not wanting their children or grandchildren to experience the 'burden' of wealth (Schervish and Herman, 1988).

The notion of altruism and self-benefit representing a neat dichotomy has been critiqued as being overly simplistic (Schervish, 2009), since key motives can span both perspectives. Impact, in its various guises, frequently tops lists of motives cited by HNWIs. For example, the 2021 Bank of America study of high-networth philanthropy (Osili et al, 2021) found that for this group, the top three motives for giving were a belief in the mission of an organisation, a belief that their gift could make a difference and a sense of personal satisfaction and fulfilment. The first two motives could be argued to be altruistic, while the third provides the donor with some psychological benefits.

So, do we unselfishly pursue maximum gain for others or do we get a personal benefit from the feelings of enhanced personal competence and achievement that result from giving? This matters because the meaning that individuals derive will be different in each case, and thus the language and approach that we use to encourage each experience of philanthropy will need to be differentiated.

The task is further complicated when one considers that the need to create impact for recipient communities is in some sense intuitive, yet the notion that benefits can accrue to the donor, and that these too can be maximised, is not. This is particularly the case where the benefits derived for the donor are psychological in nature. Encouraging greater participation in philanthropy might thus require the stimulation of a journey of self-discovery where additional sources of meaning and meaningfulness can be explicitly primed and explored.

The way in which philanthropy is experienced and the psychological benefits that may accrue are remarkably underresearched (Sargeant and Shang, 2010). Much of the previous research on how HNWIs and UHNWIs practise philanthropy has explored the topic through the lens of the impact that philanthropy can create for focal communities. Although the creation of community impact can be one source of meaning that people experience, it is only one output of a potentially more sophisticated meaning creation process. Meaning can also be created as people interact with the communities they care about, receiving warmth, support, friendship and ultimately, perhaps, entry to the community itself, becoming part of it or feeling at one with it. The ability to share these wider aspects of self was not something that was intuitive to our philanthropists as they embarked on their philanthropic journeys. Yet previous research has not provided much insight into how the experience of sharing might be supported.

Without further research to help prepare those new to the field, these additional sources of meaning can only emerge unexpectedly from direct experience of the philanthropic journey itself. In essence, the discovery of meaning is subject to the operation of random chance. Individuals may or may not encounter all the sources of meaning that should have been available to them. We hope that our research will provide philanthropists with a much better road map to navigate the experience of meaning in their philanthropy so that they can shape the most meaningful journeys possible for both themselves and their focal communities.

## Study aims

Fundamentally, we sought to explore what prompts HNWIs and UHNWIs to begin their philanthropic journey and what sustains them as they face obstacles and challenges along the way. We also sought to explore the relationship between the philanthropist's sense of self and what that self chooses to do in its philanthropy. The study further addresses the meaning individuals derive from philanthropy and what philanthropists discover to be meaningful as their journey progresses. Finally, the study addresses the role of the unknown in the experience of that meaning and the contribution it might make to the development of an individual's sense of self.

## Why is it important to study these questions?

Firstly, the answers can provide an additional perspective from which to address the current debate about whether philanthropy benefits others or the self.

If people define who they are based on a collective, such as a community, instead of a singular entity, then the distinction between benefiting others and benefiting the self ceases to have meaning. Benefiting others *is* benefiting the self. Following the same line of reasoning, when people define their singular self based on a collective, the concept of altruism is similarly redundant, because one can no longer benefit others to the exclusion of the self. The lack of any research into HNWIs' and UHNWIs' sense of self makes it impossible to draw clear conceptual distinctions in many of the sector's current debates. Is altruism still a useful concept for describing engagement in philanthropy? Should giving be driven by the presence or absence of self? We hope to provide clarity by applying new psychological lenses to inform this debate.

Secondly, it can provide an additional set of tools HNWIs and UHNWIs can use to aid their decision-making processes.

The sharp contrast between the large body of work addressing how to create, measure and maximise impact for focal communities and the much smaller body of literature addressing how to create, measure and maximise the impact on philanthropists is noteworthy. In all the literature we explored, we were unable to find a single study that identified self-defined challenges that people need to overcome in order to succeed in their philanthropy. As will later become apparent, at the start of their journey, our philanthropists were largely unaware of what these challenges might be. So, revealing something of their nature and complexity could help others to better reflect on what to expect and to make more informed decisions. In simple terms, learning from the experiences of others can equip philanthropists new to the field with the knowledge and skills necessary to overcome key challenges. This is important because the degree of challenge experienced can only intensify when individuals truly care about the impact they want to create.

Thirdly, a deeper understanding of people's sense of self can help us understand how they can create deeper meaning for themselves and others.

What is personally meaningful for a singular self is not the same as what is personally meaningful for a collective self. By definition, if people's sense of self includes the people they help, then what is meaningful for the personal self will also be meaningful for the collective. Significant research already exists pertaining to how people experience meaning and meaningfulness in their personal lives and wealth accumulation processes. However, little is known about how people experience meaning in their philanthropy, with the notable exception of early work conducted by Paul Schervish and colleagues around the turn of the century (Schervish and Herman, 1988; Schervish and Havens, 2002; Schervish et al, 2005; Schervish, 2006, 2007, 2008, 2009; Schervish and Whitaker, 2010). We also acknowledge the more recent work of Maclean et al (2015). These studies point to the importance of understanding how people experience their sense of self in the context of a moral biography and how the development of identity narratives can potentially contribute to the meaning an individual can experience.

No research, however, has clarified how people take psychological ownership of their philanthropic processes and domains and maximise the meaning derived from them. We also understand little about the role of deeply held personal beliefs in the selection of 'appropriate' philanthropy and the extent to which philanthropists incorporate these beliefs into the essence of who they are or who they were born to be. A deeper understanding of all these processes can create additional resources for HNWIs and UHNWIs and, thus, help them reach a deeper level of meaningfulness by carrying out more meaningful philanthropy.

## Methodology

To address the issues discussed, we conducted 48 semi-structured interviews with a mixture of HNWIs and UHNWIs.

Our interviews were each around one hour in duration, although some early interviewees agreed to a follow-up interview, which allowed time for reflection and exploration of the topics raised by the first interview. Memorandums were also kept, detailing the interactions with our study participants that were not part of the interview process – for example, telephone calls and digital communications. All interviews were recorded and transcribed.

Our set of semi-structured interview questions was based on the decoding-the-discipline approach used in expert interviews (Sargeant and Shang, 2016). The aim of this approach is to deconstruct what is 'obvious' to experts and, thus, provide more granular guidance to others. This was particularly appropriate as we focused on the most difficult challenges that the interviewees needed to overcome in their wealth accumulation and philanthropic journeys.

In every case, the predesigned questions were supplemented by spontaneously generated probing or prompting questions (Adler et al, 2017). Emergent themes and questions were added to the interview agenda throughout the data collection period. To supplement the interviews, additional information was collected, including publicly available information about the individuals and their organisations. This included information from newspaper articles, their personal and organisational social media activities, their enterprises' and philanthropic organisations' websites and the books they themselves and/or their associates have written. Some interviewees also shared brochures and other strategic and reflective documents. Emails and WhatsApp messages were also analysed where relevant. Permission was sought for the inclusion of these artefacts in our research.

We adopted a grounded theory approach to our data collection and analysis procedures (Glaser, 1992; Strauss and Corbin, 1998; Locke, 2001). This was appropriate given the exploratory nature of our research. The analysis thus took place alongside ongoing data collection and was highly iterative (Locke et al, 2022). Throughout the process, the extant research was also woven into our analysis and, where relevant, treated as an additional informant.

## Participants

All our interviewees have at least $1 million in liquid assets. More than half of our participants have higher than $20 million in such assets. Our sample was 64 per cent male and 36 per cent female. The age profile and geographic locations of our participants are provided in Tables 1.1 and 1.2, respectively.

Interviewees were selected because they had engaged in substantive philanthropic activities in addition to their wealth accumulation activities. Our interviewees use many definitions for that philanthropy, and these reflect the range of definitions used in the academy, as described by Sulek:

*Literal:* Encompassing references to the literal meaning of philanthropy in ancient Greek as the love of humankind.

**Table 1.1:** Age profile of interviewees

| Age category | Percentage |
| --- | --- |
| 40 and under | 19 |
| 41–59 | 25 |
| 60 and over | 56 |

**Table 1.2:** Geographic location of interviewees

| Location | Percentage |
| --- | --- |
| North and South America | 40 |
| Europe | 35 |
| Asia-Pacific | 15 |
| Middle East and North Africa | 10 |

*Archaic:* For usages now considered largely obsolete, such as those referring to philanthropy as the 'love of god for humankind' or as being synonymous with 'humanity.'

*Ideal:* To describe the attainment of ideal aims, goals, outcomes, or objectives in terms of meeting a need, attaining a good, and/or advancing human happiness and well-being.

*Ontological:* To describe an innate desire, moral sentiment, psychological predisposition, or other such aspect of human nature that impels people to want to help others.

*Volitional:* To describe the good will, intent, or readiness to voluntarily help others.

*Actual:* To describe an objective act, such as giving of money, time, or effort, to a charitable cause or public purpose.

> *Social:* To describe a relation, movement, organization,
> or other such social entity larger than the individual
> that embodies an explicitly defined charitable cause
> or good. (2010, p 204, italics in original)

To illustrate, our interviewees define philanthropy as their love
for others, a channel of God's love for others, the attainment
of moral ideals, an innate desire to be who they were created
to be, goodwill or an act that created a new social reality for
the collective good. Some of our interviewees express their
philanthropy by making monetary contributions in the forms of
one-off, sustaining or legacy gifts, while others also volunteer their
time, sometimes serving on the boards of focal initiatives. Many of
them give through their businesses' corporate social responsibility
programmes or have founded their own for-purpose organisations,
non-profit organisations and family or individual foundations.

A diverse range of opinions were expressed. We found
differences in:

- what systemic changes should be prioritised;
- where they stood on rights issues;
- how they viewed the purpose of philanthropy in their
  focal community;
- how they prioritised and negotiated potential trade-offs between
  their responsibilities in the local versus the global community;
- what time frame they think their philanthropy should function
  in – for example, whether they should spend down their wealth
  during their lifetime or leave wealth to outlive them and carry
  on into future generations;
- what long-term impact they think their philanthropic
  endeavours should aim to make.

The diversity in our interviewees' philanthropic experience lends
itself to the discovery of a deeper, more holistic set of observations
about key sources of meaning in philanthropy and what may be
experienced as meaningful by individuals.

In respect of wealth accumulation, many of our interviewees
describe themselves as entrepreneurs. As was the case for definitions
of philanthropy, they define entrepreneurship in a way that is

very similar to how the term is defined in the academy. It is a multifaceted process (Davidsson et al, 2001). It 'is the initiation, engagement, and performance of entrepreneurial endeavours embedded in environmental conditions, where an entrepreneurial endeavour is the investment of resources (i.e., cognitive, behavioural, financial, and/or other resources) into the pursuit (exploration and/or exploitation) of a potential opportunity' (Shepherd et al, 2019, p 161).

A central facet of the definition by Shepherd et al is the application of resources. Our interviewees' perspectives on resources show similarities with extant research in the sense that resources are seen to include not only financial resources but many other forms as well. These include time, talent, energy, social networks and influence. When using the term 'opportunity', they refer to not only market opportunities but also opportunities to create collective good for themselves and others in their community. Many of our interviewees practise their entrepreneurship in a way that delivers this dual bottom line, either by adding societal value directly (for example, through the creation of renewable energy sources) or indirectly (for example, through the creation of a non-profit to help commercial banks reach new markets and thus increase access to capital). It therefore makes no sense to consider interviewees' entrepreneurial journeys as somehow separate from journeys in philanthropy. Some certainly are. But for many of our interviewees, the two are deeply interconnected and could even be experienced as one holistic journey to do good in a community. It is therefore no surprise that, as we will later illustrate, the meaning derived from one experience of self can have a profound influence and impact on the meaning from other experiences of self.

## Book structure

The rest of the text is organised in the following way.

In Chapter 2, we define two key concepts that have been used repeatedly by our interviewees to describe the nature of their philanthropic experiences: *psychological ownership* (that is, 'that state in which individuals feel as though the target of ownership (material or immaterial in nature) or a piece of it is "theirs"' (Pierce et al, 2001, p 299); and *moral conviction* (that is, a strong and absolute belief or attitude that something is right or wrong, moral or immoral; Skitka et al, 2021). Specifically, our interviewees differentiate the ownership they experience over domain from the ownership they experience over process. The purpose of the chapter is not to superficially conclude that everyone takes ownership over their philanthropy or everyone considers moral conviction important. To the contrary, we use these concepts to illustrate how diverse our interviewees' philanthropic experiences are. Whether they take ownership and experience moral conviction, how they experience these processes and what they ultimately experience are all different for our interviewees. So how can we understand and support people's philanthropic journeys in the face of such differences? To best answer that question, we must develop a deeper level of analysis, looking at the person behind the giving and thus who the person is who is taking psychological ownership and deciding on moral conviction. We begin that journey in Chapter 2.

In Chapter 3, we define the notion of *self*. We define three types of identity that people can label themselves with: moral identity; personal identity; and relational identity. We also provide examples of how these different forms of identity can be expressed through giving. We do not offer any prescriptions here about the kind of definition of the self that will create the most meaningful philanthropy. Rather, we learn that to explore meaning, it is first necessary to understand how people choose which labels they want to use to define themselves (in different situations) and how they define what these labels mean to them. In Chapter 3, we also lay the foundation for all the psychological vocabulary we require for the balance of the book.

In Chapter 4, we take our discussion of people's sense of self to the next level and describe a particular self-transformation process that can provide a rich source of meaning for an individual's philanthropy: *identity ceding*. Identity ceding is defined as a psychological process through which people willingly allow their sense of self to be transformed in order to achieve the goals they share with a community. Identity ceding can be experienced in five different elements of self: the agentic self; the object self; the experiential self; the represented self; and the meta-self. We define these terms and explain how they link together to provide a holistic sense of self. Chapter 4 is by far the most conceptually challenging chapter in this book. It is also where the central thesis of the book begins to emerge. In it, we describe the pivotal connection between what people do in their philanthropy, who they are as a person and how they relate to the community in which their philanthropy is grounded.

In Chapter 5, we focus on a particular form of self, the *essential self* – that is, who our philanthropists believe they truly are, were born to be or are meant to be. We define what the essential self is and then explain how this essential self can be experienced, developed and expressed in the context of one's philanthropy. We also explore how identity ceding can enhance processes related to the essential self and how the essential self is experienced in the five elements of self.

In Chapter 6, we extend our discussion into *meaning* and *meaningfulness*. We explain that meaning is experienced not only as the sense we make of something or what it signifies, but also as the process through which the sense is made. Similarly, meaningfulness derives not only from how significant we judge our experiences to be, but also from the process of allowing this sense of significance to emerge over time. We begin by exploring these concepts in the context of what people do in their philanthropy and the impact they create. We then look at how meaning can also be experienced in association with people's object self, agentic self and meta-self. We suggest that by decoding the process of how self-related meaning can be created during one's philanthropic journey, we can nurture its emergence and potentially unlock more substantial engagement. Philanthropy released this way will create more impact for communities and greater meaning and meaningfulness for the philanthropists that made that impact possible.

In Chapter 7, we outline additional paths to meaningful philanthropy by leveraging the learning we have derived so far. We cover the concepts of authenticity, transcendence, self-efficacy, self-worth and coherence. We also differentiate identity ceding from general self-transcendence and specify the directionality that is inherent in philanthropic decisions. Then we explore why these paths to meaningful philanthropy can help sustain philanthropic journeys in the long term, how they can help families create the most meaningful philanthropic journeys for each individual family member and how one's philanthropic experience can enhance the meaning and purpose that one can ascribe to one's life.

We conclude in Chapter 8 with a set of answers to questions that can help the individual reflect on their philanthropy, and we outline the additional understanding that could be delivered by further research. We also provide a set of action steps, based on the recommendations from this research, that people who are contemplating their own philanthropic journeys can take.

Case histories from our real-world examples are used throughout the text to help bring all these academic concepts to life and demonstrate their practical relevance.

2

# Psychological ownership and moral conviction

Many of our interviewees find it difficult to discuss what their wealth accumulation or wealth distribution experience means for them without referencing their sense of who they are. But referring to the 'self' is not the only language they use to describe these experiences. Instead, they can default to the language of what the literature regards as psychological ownership and moral conviction. In this chapter, we first define these terms and then explore how they apply to our study.

## Psychological ownership

*Psychological ownership* is defined as 'that state in which individuals feel as though the target of ownership (material or immaterial in nature) or a piece of it is "theirs"' (Pierce et al, 2001, p 299). When people take ownership of an activity, they may say, for example: 'I own the vision of this company'; 'I built this company, led it and grew it to today's scale'; 'I take ownership of this company's success'. Some are equally open about taking ownership of their failures and how they learned or grew from them.

This sense of ownership has also been articulated in previous studies of entrepreneurs, although not necessarily HNWIs or UHNWIs. Grimes (2018), for example, asked 59 business founders to tell him about their entrepreneurial ideas. He found that '[t]he entrepreneurs consistently referred to particular moments in time in which the ideas were "sparked" or "birthed."' (Grimes, 2018, p 1698). The entrepreneurs considered these ideas 'not just as creative projects tied to abstract economic opportunities, but as reflections of their personal values and beliefs, which ultimately contributed to a sense of psychological ownership' regarding a venture (Grimes, 2018, p 1698).

People can experience a sense of ownership of something without necessarily articulating which part of them is owning it. When people say something like 'I own the vision of this company', they don't specifically articulate whether it is the entrepreneur in them or the father or the churchgoer who owns the vision. Although discussions about ownership can be helpful in securing new levels of meaning, this level of reflection was not common among our interviewees. This is a theme that we return to later.

In this chapter, we focus on one of the most significant differences that our interviewees were commonly aware of in their experience of psychological ownership: the distinction between ownership of *domain* and *process*.

- By domain, our interviewees typically refer to the domain in which they choose to operate. It describes the 'what' of what they do. The business domains our philanthropists have chosen to operate in are as diverse as sustainable energy, healthcare, real estate, financial services, car sales and online gaming. Their selection of domain is highly expressive of their sense of self, there having to be a fit between the 'what' of the activity and the 'who' of who they are.
- By process, our interviewees typically refer to the method they use to achieve their goals and how they measure their outputs or outcomes. It describes the 'how' of what they do. In the business domain, processes include the way they recruit, train, mentor, lead and care for their employees, how they leverage their connections to make something new happen and how they help create new ecosystems that are conducive to the creation of entrepreneurial success. We found the 'how' to be equally expressive of 'who' people are. Most are purposeful in their selections, wanting to do things 'their way' even when they aren't sure from the outset what 'their way' is.

## Moral conviction

We also found evidence of moral conviction in the selection of domains and process.

A conviction is an unshakable belief in something, without the need for proof or evidence. *Moral conviction*, therefore, refers to a strong and absolute belief or attitude that something is right or wrong, moral or immoral (Skitka et al, 2021). It turns out that these moral attitudes are comparatively immune to external influences from, for example, one's respected authority figures, one's peers, one's subordinates and even market pressure. And moral convictions are important because they give rise to an intense motivational force that in extremis (in other contexts, such as campaigning) can border on violence (Skitka and Mullen, 2002).

Among our interviewees, different levels of moral conviction are present in the choices made about both domains and processes. The choice of each could be driven by a belief not only that the activity is right for them, but also that it is right in the moral sense.

Similar to their experience of psychological ownership, our interviewees do not necessarily reflect on any differences between the moral convictions of different aspects of self. Generic imperatives related to how they choose to live their life and what is right in a particular context can be used to mask sometimes significant differences between the various selves that are in focus. Greater reflection on which self is at the table and, thus, more awareness of what is seen as moral by each self can give rise to significant psychological dissonance and discomfort. It is, therefore, easy to understand why people don't always carry out this sort of self-reflection – engaging with this level of complexity isn't always worth the effort in a given decision situation. Unfortunately, when situations arise where such analysis is unavoidable, people find themselves inexperienced and ill-equipped to handle this reflection effectively. We explore these situations in greater detail in later chapters.

Some interviewees experience a sense of moral conviction in how they choose their domain. In business, in order for them to call a domain *theirs*, they have to be able to articulate the collective good created by their enterprise. They have to be able to say how their business contributes to, for example, the increased use of

**Figure 2.1:** Ownership and moral conviction

|  |  | Moral conviction | |
|---|---|---|---|
|  |  | Yes | No |
| Ownership | Domain |  |  |
|  | Process |  |  |

renewable energy, the adoption of healthcare products that can save lives or the design of financial products that serve the needs of people from disadvantaged communities. For other interviewees, there is no moral conviction per se; their business is simply something that they build to create wealth for their families and others they care about. For reasons that we explain later, when all else is equal, psychologists believe that people experience a greater sense of meaningfulness when they have a moral conviction associated with what they choose to do.

Whether interviewees consider the domain of their business moral or not, some of them experience a sense of moral conviction in terms of the method they use to achieve their business goals and how they measure their outputs or outcomes. Some consider the support of their local economy and the provision of job opportunities through their business a moral matter, regardless of what business they are in. Others consider making the largest possible difference in the lives of their employees, while creating the greatest possible business success in their chosen domain, a moral matter. What is considered morally 'right' differs from one person to another. There are no absolute or universal prescriptions for what is moral and what is not. A matrix in which different scenarios can be positioned is depicted in Figure 2.1.

## Taking ownership and experiencing moral conviction in philanthropy

While we have so far been discussing the wealth generation activities our interviewees have engaged with, the same system of classification appears as relevant to interviewees' philanthropic experiences in that they share the sense that there is a type of philanthropy that they can call *theirs* and that they can declare psychological ownership over.

Similar to the entrepreneurial activities discussed earlier, people differentiate their ownership of domains from their ownership of processes. For some people, the choice of which domains to focus on is deeply important to them. Deviating from these causes would not be acceptable. For example, they may be committed to reducing the suffering of farm animals, helping orphans who suffer extreme poverty or helping create infrastructure to support local entrepreneurs. Some interviewees note that navigating their philanthropic landscape in order to identify just the right domain areas for them is the most important decision they have made to date. Everything else is seen as flowing from this critical decision.

For others, the choice of domain is less important than how they choose to practise philanthropy in that domain. Typical concerns discussed by our interviewees include the following:

- where they stand on how much risk philanthropy should absorb;
- how much they value trust in creating philanthropic impact;
- the degree to which they would like science-based evidence to guide their practice;
- the amount of resources they are willing to deploy for the impact they create;
- whether an organisation is built on the correct management and leadership foundation;
- whether they have leveraged the resources available to them in the best possible way.

Illustrations from interviewees P1 and P2 provide a flavour of how our interviewees experience ownership of domains and ownership of processes, as well as how their views can be markedly different.

## Ownership of domains and processes: the case of P1 and P2

P1 founded an organisation to help others practise effective altruism. He pinpointed what has been most personally meaningful for him in this journey and shared how he differentiates *his* domains and processes.

'I think that's where I found real satisfaction in the success that [the organisation I co-founded] has now, in leveraging way more resources than we have ourselves and having had that vision and bringing that to reality. I think that's where the real source of satisfaction and purpose comes from. About six or seven years ago, I came into contact with the effective altruism movement, and as an entrepreneur that really resonated with me, because it was basically very similar to entrepreneurship. You know, you use your resources to create the most successful company, make as much money as possible, etc., and effective altruism was very much doing that [maximising the social good created with resources].'

When asked what element of that journey that he found most satisfying, he said:

'I like getting the biggest effect for my resources. I get a lot of satisfaction out of maximising. With my entrepreneurship, we had only limited resources of funding and support, so I had to leverage what I had into building a successful business. And then with these [philanthropic] opportunities, it's exactly the same. It's looking at the resources I have available and how could I really maximise the expected social good, the impact of those resources, and optimising that gives me the greatest satisfaction. Obviously, underlying that is this feeling that I'm positively contributing to a better world, and potentially significantly, but it's really about using limited resources to have the biggest sort of effect.'

He was then asked if the domain where that leveraging happens is important in terms of whether something feels more or less satisfying. He said:

'No, not really, because my initial philanthropic focus was very much global health and development, alleviating poverty and suffering. And, if you see what I do now, it's very much meta-funding, building the ecosystem, which is very indirect, you know. You can't say I've saved so many lives or I've sent so many girls to school. It's much less concrete, and yet, for me, it's a lot more satisfying. I know it leads to better results, because it's way less direct but it's way more impactful.'

He also commented on whether, from his personal perspective, he needs to see the ripple effect, or if he could simply trust that the ripple effect exists:

'It has to be carefully assessed, but it's not like I need to see it directly, because, obviously, the chain of events is much longer in what we are doing now. But I know it's substantiated. I know that there's a huge multiplier, because I see the grants that they're [the organisation I co-founded] directing now and I know the sort of impact those grants are expected to have. It's focused on highly leveraged, high-risk, high-return philanthropy, so it's less concrete, but in expectation, it's way more impactful. So, it's a sort of careful assessment and the sort of belief that all this is achieving a lot more than when I was doing very direct stuff.'

Reflecting on what, in terms of the creation of the organisation he co-founded, he finds to be the most personally meaningful, he said:

'So, getting the right people involved and then helping create it – kicking it off. That was the most meaningful. And then I was able to exit, so I'm no longer actively involved in the organisation. It's now running independently, and I think that's a positive. I look for things that can eventually run on independently of me, so I can refocus my energy on something else, sort of envisioning and creating the early stage of the next venture.'

While, for P1, starting an initiative is a process he can take ownership of, for others, growing an entity and bringing its activities to scale may hold more allure or represent a better fit with what is uniquely theirs.

Across the spectrum of interviewees, people have ended up in quite different places as they have sought out what is uniquely theirs. This is illustrated by P2's experience. P2's father created her family's wealth, and P2 is now managing her family's philanthropy. The family members are also searching for what is uniquely theirs in terms of causes and processes, but their search may lead them down a different path than that taken by P1. P2 said:

> 'If you're trying to impact heart disease, there's so many factors – there's obesity, there's poverty, there's social factors. If you go hit any one of those, you're probably making an impact. It's going to be hard to measure the impact of your specific intervention, because heart disease is complex and you can't impact all risk factors, but just because it's not a measurable impact doesn't mean it's not worth doing it.
>
> You have to run with your gut a little bit more ... there are times when you know you just have to trust that it's making an impact, even if it's not immediately apparent.
>
> It may seem like a vanity metric, but if you contribute to an organisation you believe in, and you write a cheque and they're out there making an impact, then, at the very worst case, your impact is their impact. No, it's not perfect, and it's not what we are striving for, but it's nice to know that even if you can't see the long-term impact of your effort, there is a direct impact. We strive for systemic change but see direct impact with non-profit groups as a means to our end. Those groups engage in their communities. They do good work and live their world.'

When asked whether, when she is in the philanthropic space, measuring impact delivers as high a level of satisfaction as listening to her gut, she said:

> 'This is a conversation we've had among our board actually, and there is a comment like "we need to

run like a business, not as a philanthropy". That sounds great, because there's some really poorly run philanthropies out there. But there's also some really poorly run businesses, and I think the objective shouldn't be qualified by an organisation's tax status.

Motivation and purpose are at the crux of any organisation. Even the most successful private businesses don't claim profit as the reason why they do something, but they use it as a measurement of their impact; whether or not it's the only or ... the most important measurement is in the eye of the beholder. A philanthropy doesn't have the luxury of that simplicity. It can measure its success by the amount of funding distributed, but without understanding the trickle-down impact, it's a pretty shallow metric. The trick is picking a point that is further downstream than the cheque but not so far that you aren't around to see it. You run the risk of being very complacent and just writ[ing] your cheques and feel[ing] lovely about it, warm and fuzzy, and then just walking away.

And that's not the way that we, and certainly I, ever intended to operate. You never want to be dumb money. But philanthropy and business are different. In business, you have to keep reacting to market conditions and keeping up the fast pace. And then when you get into philanthropy, that's not what you're trying to do. Your role isn't to beat the market; your role is to fill a gap in the market.

We've had these discussions in some of our grant determinations. There was one recently where we were asked to fund an accessible playground that allows for engaging play for kids with a wide range of physical and cognitive abilities. So, there were, like, 12 kids in the class who would benefit from this. The rest of the school didn't need a playground built to that spec, but for those 12 kids, it would be huge. So, the school district won't fund this, because it makes no financial sense, and the private sector's not going to come in and do it, because there's no profit in it, but that's when we can come in and do it.'

What P1 and P2 discovered is what is uniquely *their* philanthropic way of being. They choose domains and processes that are uniquely theirs. Treading any other path would simply not work for them, because that is not who they are. Although neither of them need to spell out who they are to explore the fit, they have the conviction and the intuition that what they have found is theirs and is right for them.

Many interviewees share the same perspective as P1 and P2. Some of them, similar to P2, use their philanthropy to satisfy the needs of just a few, while others, like P1, want to do the most good for as many people as possible. Equally, some interviewees loath the sentiment of running a charity like a business, while others see it as the only way their philanthropy can properly function.

We also found that some of our interviewees initially felt comfortable with their philanthropy, while others searched for a decade or longer before they could feel truly comfortable with its nature and see it as a fit with their strongly held convictions. Yet others are still searching for this degree of comfort. The experiences of P3 and P4 reflect the diversity of this search process.

## Fit with strongly held beliefs: the case of P3 and P4

For P3, her early entrepreneurial ventures reflected her system of moral convictions. They served a purpose that she cares passionately about, they gave her the opportunity to live out her business curiosity and creativity, and they provided her with the wealth she needed to embark on her later philanthropic journey. She described her wealth accumulation activity in the following way:

'I think I've been an entrepreneur my whole life. You know, you kind of start with the lemonade stand and move from there. But my first real business was a medical market research firm that was predicated on helping physician processes and pharmaceutical companies navigate the patient journey.

So I did everything from advisory boards to medical market research around the world. I really looked at the best patient models.

My sole purpose when I started that business was … I always used to say I wanted Mr Jones to live long enough to see his son's wedding, because I saw patients falling through the cracks in our healthcare system.

And so I went above and beyond, and I mean nights, weekends, multiple planes a day, in order to try to figure out the right model. And then to teach that model to other folks around the country and around the world to try to enhance patient care.

It sounds easier than it was. In reality, it's kind of a never-ending struggle, rather like the hunt for world peace! But it was incredibly helpful, and I learned a ton. And we did good work. I really do think Mr Jones got to see his son's wedding because [of] a lot of the things we put into place, which was very cool.'

P3's domain is to create market research that can help improve patients' life expectancy and quality of life. She went through extensive research, spanning over a decade, to find the right process that she considers uniquely hers. These include an element that she particularly enjoys – providing training programmes for surgeons to help them better understand their patients' journeys. She cannot hide her excitement when she takes personal ownership in the wins that she considers to be related to her moral conviction.

'I mean every time I saw one of our patient charts being used … that really did mean that the patient was getting care to the fullest extent. That was a personal win.

My whole career has been predicated on creating new models or seeing change. So, you know, when I taught change management and more efficient medical models, it always gave me excitement.

In one case, we developed a national programme where we taught a community-based urologist how to treat patients, and we would get the entire base of community groups all rowing in the same direction. That doesn't sound difficult. But you're dealing with very smart surgeons who never went to school to become a part of multiple groups; they went to school to sculpt their individual performance. That's doctors in general. So getting them aligned and watching a new group or a cohort succeed, and a system just fall into place for better medical healthcare ... I just thought it was cool. I still think it's the coolest thing I do.'

For P3, the purpose of her business is to serve the patients who need help. Although she has a long family tradition of giving back, and she has practised philanthropy since the age of seven, she did not seek out a philanthropic opportunity to give back in a substantive way until she realised a chunk of her wealth through the sale of her first business. For P3, her philanthropic experience naturally progressed from her business activities. They all serve a coherent whole, which she considers to be morally right, intellectually exciting and personally fulfilling. Collectively (and as domains and processes), they are all consistent with what she regards as the North Star in her life. And all move her forward in that rewarding direction.

P4's search for his "virtuous" cycle takes a slightly different form. It involves his primary business activity, which spans over 35 years, in the fossil fuel sector. When asked to think about the very first activity he would characterise as the beginning of his entrepreneurship journey and the purpose he set out to achieve in that experience, P4 said:

'I think it's very hard to identify a specific activity [as the beginning of my entrepreneurship journey]. I think it's a mindset where you have an interest or desire and you want to pursue that because you believe that is where an opportunity set lies and you're willing to (a) buck conventional wisdom and (b) have an idea. And especially when you're young, you have limited downside in pursuing that idea, so you pursue that idea.

For me, I didn't fully understand the commodity space, but I thought about commodities as a global product that was needed by everyone and, therefore, will always be in demand. And how did I fit into that cycle? And that is how I got into the space.'

Similar to P3, P4 found his space in the energy industry by asking what the needs should be met by commodities and how he could fit into that cycle. He also is looking for opportunities where his ideas can buck the conventional wisdom and make a difference. He said what has kept him at the entity he has been with for over 30 years

'was never to be rich, because I'm not sure what that means. It was a challenge to take advantage of the opportunities presented to me, and I never really doubted the path that I was on. And I never really doubted that that would lead to flexibility, financial flexibility, down the road, and to live that flexibility well.'

When asked how he would characterise living that flexibility well, he said, "having the flexibility to provide comfortably for your family, but also having the financial flexibility to support other causes that interest you and that you feel you can make a difference to".

Some of these differences he chose to make in a for-profit capacity when he built the only private subsea data network across the Atlantic. Of this initiative, he said:

'I have since sold that and it's now a private company. But, you know, it's about having the conviction [taking ownership] to be able to deliver that. And the journey isn't easy, but the conviction is there. And the reward is that you have financial gains which you can then do what you will with.

I'm not very interested in going out and driving fast cars or being flashy, however you define flashy, but I'm interested in supporting causes which I think are interesting. One is around journalism, two is around environmental sustainability, partially because I'm in the energy business so I feel like in order to maintain equilibrium, I need to be balanced in my view. And the third area where I'm spending a lot of time and money is in education. I'd like to believe that by involving myself in those organisations, I've helped them transform their mission, because I've given them the financial flexibility to be able to deliver that.'

His support of these causes is not only important to the causes themselves; it is also important to what he takes ownership of in his moral conviction. P4 said:

'With themes that I think are important – sustainability, there is something very virtuous about a full cycle. I was in the energy business. I believe energy is essential for evolving basic life. We need energy to live, but I also recognise the side effects of that – so what can I do to mitigate those side effects and what can I do to facilitate better energy? Creating carbon sinks, creating more efficient, for example, fuel stoves in Africa, are things that I think can help on the margin, and [that] I've been involved with.

The other thing is this whole news and information. I am shocked, especially in my travels, as to how partisan and polar the news organisations are and how we how we look at those. Yeah, I think it's just sort of common themes that have that have run through my environment for a long time, and they, again, feel very natural to me.'

The virtuous cycle is what P4 takes ownership of and what he considers to be morally right for him. As noted earlier, his virtuous cycle encompasses his major business activities, spanning 30 years, as well his business investment activities and his various philanthropic ventures. So in some senses his journey is similar to that of P3, whose virtuous cycle is self-contained within her entrepreneurial activities and grew from the domain (medical care) and processes (globalisation and specialised training) that she owns. Through the financial flexibility P4 obtained, he is now providing for other people, and he aims to find solutions for the problems that he encounters through his work, through his philanthropy.

The complexity in how people experience psychological ownership and moral conviction within their wealth accumulation activities determines, to a certain extent, how they experience psychological ownership and moral conviction in their philanthropic activities. When asked how they consider the differences between their own and others' philanthropic approaches, some interviewees simply state that they prefer their way and would not practise their philanthropy in any other way. At no point do they raise their preferences to the level of moral rights or wrongs. But other interviewees do, noting that their way is the morally right way and that other ways are morally inferior.

The philosophical debate about which way is considered, objectively, universally moral is beyond the scope of this research. Some, may choose moral relativism to provide their guiding moral principles, while others may call on the moral absolutes laid down by a loving God. It is important to understand that the lens of moral conviction research is respectful of everyone's ability to define what is morally right or wrong for themselves.

## Conclusion

In this chapter, we have explored questions related to how people define the various paths available to them and how they select the paths that are uniquely theirs. We have also explored the distinction between domains and processes, noting that both can provide powerful sources of meaning, particularly when they align with the individual's moral convictions. Our examples demonstrated that interviewees have multiple perspectives on morality, but the additional utility offered by alignment between that morality and their selected paths is available to all.

We have also flagged the potential difficulty of examining moral conviction as though it spans, universally, all the identities that make up our self concept. If different aspects of self have different perspectives, conflicts can result, significantly impeding any wellbeing that might otherwise accrue from philanthropic activities. To more fully explore this and other issues, we must now reflect more on the nature of the individual or the self behind the philanthropy. This is the focus of Chapter 3.

3

# The self

It was apparent to us early on just how much 'self' was at the core of the journeys our philanthropists experienced. While at the outset, their goal may have been primarily to help others, the manner in which that goal was manifest reflects a deep sense of what is theirs to 'own' in the philanthropic space and how that might fit with their sense of who they are. As their journey progresses, many philanthropists find that they could allow that sense of self to morph to deliver additional impact for the focal community. They discover too that this journey in self could create additional sources of meaning that could nourish them in ways they had not previously considered.

In this chapter, we explore a little of that journey. We begin, though, with a definition of self.

## Defining self

The self, defined as our sense of who we are, may be the most important and most researched topic in psychology (Legrand and Ruby, 2009). According to a variety of academics, our sense of who we are can be defined by:

- what we think and how we feel (Mischel and Shoda, 1995);
- what we do (Buss and Craik, 1983);
- what we have (Belk, 1988);
- who we are in relationships with (Andersen and Chen, 2002);
- which culture we live in (Markus and Kitayama, 1991);

- which social category we belong (Tajfel and Turner, 2004);
- who we choose to fuse our sense of self with (Swann et al, 2012).

Individual interviewees described their sense of self in most, but not necessarily all, these different ways.

It is important to recognise that people's sense of self has multiple components. People have a range of identities (Markus and Wurf, 1987), and it is in the integration and prioritisation of these identities that they discover what their lives are for and, in terms of the topic of our research, the purposes that entrepreneurship and philanthropy may have for them. It is also important to understand that people's sense of self is not fixed. It can change over time, being shaped by the experiences of daily life (a bottom–up process) or by continual reflection and evaluation of how relevant a given activity is to one's sense of self (a top-down process).

## Moral, personal and relational identity

We primarily explored three components of the self in our research: moral identity; personal identity; and relational identity. We focused on these particular identities because they are the identities most commonly articulated by our interviewees. We illustrate how the choices people make in integrating and prioritising these identities help define who they are and what philanthropy means for them.

### Moral identity

Moral identity can be defined as 'a commitment of one's sense of self to an *action* (or set of actions) that promotes or protects the welfare of others' (Hart et al, 1998, p 515). These actions can be employed to articulate who people are to themselves and who they are to others (for example, an individual might act in a certain way to tell themselves: 'I care for the less fortunate, the most marginalised, those suffering the most extreme level of poverty'). Moral identity can also be defined as a *willingness* to act in this way (Hart et al, 1998). Thus, from this perspective, people act not because they are influenced by social pressure (for example, because they think 'people in my position should practise philanthropy'), but rather because they desire to help out of their own initiative (for example, 'I practise philanthropy because I want to do it out of my own volition. I would practise it whether other people think I ought to or not. I would choose to practise it my way, irrespective of how others think I should practise it').

The third way that moral identity can be defined is as a set of moral traits shaped by a distinct mental image of what a moral person is likely to think, feel and do (Aquino and Reed, 2002). People's moral identities can vary in terms of content. Whereas one person may see being compassionate as important to their moral identity, another may emphasise being fair and just (Haidt, 2001). That said, there are some commonalities. In general, moral people are typically described as sincere, modest and fair, as well as disciplined, prudent and organised. In addition, they are good at resisting temptations (that is, they exhibit high self-control) and thinking about the future consequences of their behaviour. Finally, integrity is important to them, and they want to see themselves as possessing moral traits. Thus, moral people are:

- *modest* – they do not think they are entitled to more than others, and they do not consider themselves to be of a higher status than others;
- *honest* – they would not pretend to be someone else in order to secure favours. They would also not do anything in private that they would not do in front of others;
- *conscientious* – they plan ahead and organise things to avoid scrambling at the last minute, and they always attempt to be accurate in what they do;
- *compassionate* – they consider the needs and interests of others and how their actions affect others. They tend to experience feelings of warmth, compassion and concern for others. This is different from feeling personally distressed by others' feelings. The latter is an other-oriented feeling of concern (Davis, 1983);
- *effective at regulating behaviour* – they are capable of regulating their own behaviours effectively, so they can refrain from acting in ways that have positive short-term consequences but also negative long-term consequences. The aim is that their day-to-day behaviour will influence how things might turn out in the

future. They are willing to sacrifice their immediate happiness or wellbeing in order to achieve positive future outcomes for all (Strathman et al, 1994). They are also able to focus on long-term goals, and they are not easily tempted to slip from their high standards of behaviour (Tangney et al, 2004). They also refrain from manipulating others (Dahling et al, 2009). They do not take pleasure in controlling others, and they do not issue 'instructions' to others in interpersonal situations.

In our research with charity donors, we found that the experience of moral identity is a key driver of giving. The most commonly cited traits of a moral person, based on our research on donors, are being caring, compassionate, kind, friendly, helpful, generous, empathetic, loyal and trustworthy (Sargeant and Shang, 2017). What is interesting about this list is that all these traits have an orientation toward others, even though they are characteristics of self. Most of our interviewees would include a mixture of these words when asked to describe their sense of who they are.

P13 described her morality as her following her North Star. P4 described his morality as the formation of a "virtuous" cycle within his entrepreneurial and philanthropic activities. P1 described his morality as helping the most with the fewest resources, while for P2, it is caring for those who are left out by existing social care systems. The domains and processes that they consider theirs differ, but their experience of being someone with the conviction of a particular set of moral values is the same. They all want to do good and be a good person.

### Personal identity

There are many other ways that people experience their sense of self. They may do so through a set of characteristics that do not necessarily involve concern for others or a set of moral traits. They could simply have characteristics such as being creative, innovative, opportunistic, determined, focused, curious and flexible (Grimes, 2018; Arikan et al, 2020; Foy and Gruber, 2022). These characteristics do not require people to interact with others in order to experience them. They can simply be experienced as a lone individual.

Although the traits our interviewees refer to in describing their sense of who they are have similarities to the traits other populations use to do so, our interviewees show a stronger tendency to define their sense of who they are according to their creativity. In particular, similar to entrepreneurs in other studies, they define their creativity by the actions they take to create new products or processes (Schumpeter, 1935), enter into new markets (Lumpkin and Dess, 1996), generate networks in existing and emerging ecosystems and create new social realities (Kilby, 1971; Stevenson and Jarillo, 1990).

## Relational identity

Consistent with previous research, our interviewees also describe themselves in terms of the relationships they have and the collectives to which they belong. Psychologists call these *relational identities* or *collective identities*.

- *Relational identity* describes our identity in the context of the personal relationship that we have with a significant other (for example, 'I am the wife of my partner'; 'I am the mother of my son'; 'I am the mentor of my mentee').
- *Organisational identity* describes our identity in the context of our relationship to (or with) an organisation (for example, 'I am the founder, builder or scaler of an organisation').
- *Group identity* describes our identity in the context of our relationship with a defined group (for example, a regional or chapter member of an international network of HNWIs).
- *Social identity* describes our identity in the context of social interactions. This includes gender identity, ethnic identity and refugee identity.
- *Regional, national and international identity* describes identity in the context of one's geographic, national or international location or origin.

We have ordered these categories very deliberately to reflect intimacy. For example, the level of intimacy people experience in their relational identities will typically be higher than the intimacy they experience in their organisational or group identities. Intimacy matters because the greater the intimacy experienced, the more satisfying relationships become and the more likely it is that the identity will influence behaviour. Satisfying relationships also lead to more other-directed concerns, and the more other-directed people are in these relationships, the more satisfied they can feel if their sense of the relationship is reciprocated by others (Clark and Mills, 1979).

In most of the social category-based identities or regional and organisational identities, in which people do not experience intimacy, their behaviours are influenced by the social norms that these collectives or categories adopt. Thus, while our interviewees may adopt a leadership role, they continue to abide by relevant norms in the same way that others do. This is particularly the case during the early stages of their exploration of their entrepreneurial and philanthropic selves, when they are collecting information about what they may eventually call 'theirs' (that is, experiencing psychological ownership of their chosen domain or process).

Next, we share the experiences of three of our interviewees to explore how moral, personal and collective identities play out when HNWIs discover themselves through entrepreneurship and philanthropy.

## *Identity and its development in entrepreneurship and philanthropy: the case of P5, P6 and P7*

P5 is a second-generation wealth inheritor. She also has her own career, which has allowed her to accumulate her own wealth. She sat on the Board of Directors of her family business before she came to devote most of her time to a non-profit that one of her relatives founded. She also manages the family foundation. When asked how she defines her sense of who she is, she said her defining word is "kindness" (that is, a moral identity). She said: "If we behave in a way that makes other people behave better toward each other, it has huge impact, and you just don't know the *kind* of impact it's going to have, but it does."

When she began to explain why kindness has become so important to her, she put it in the context of the relationships she has with her family members:

> 'Historically, my family left [country] in 1959. My ancestors were refugees. Three of my four grandparents

came on a boat from [country] to [country]. I grew up in [country], so I've seen a lot of lack of access to opportunity, so I get all the reasons why we should be kind.'

Commenting on when she knew kindness was her defining identity, she said:

'I don't think I can give you one specific point in time. That's just the way we were brought up, and I think that's the right thing to do. My mother was very gentle and very kind, and just a wonderful role model. Both my parents were always very philanthropic. My dad could be very kind, but he could also be really mean. So, I can't say that he was necessarily kind to us as kids, but philanthropically he did do some really significant things, such as introducing vitamin A into the sugar of the country so that the entire population would have sufficient vitamin A and reduce the incidence of blindness. So, we're talking about a very macro-level strategy.

It's a combination of having somebody who's very strategic, very big picture and making huge bets. And, then, the very micro level of my mom, you know, just cuddling us when we were sad. You know, that kind of kindness. So, it's not a moment, it's just the influence of the environment that I grew up in.'

The history of P5's family, the cuddles that she received from her mother and her observation of her father's actions formed her views on why kindness is needed and how kindness can be lived out. However, when she lives this kindness out in her life own life, it appears as hers, not her family's, even though it may have its origins there.

'I have my way of doing it. With the non-profit organisation I chair, I'm doing something that hasn't been done before, and it can have a macro impact, which you could say I am modelling after the vitamin A thing. But it's my way, my version. When my cousin died, I took it over, and I've changed it and done it differently. It's just what you do, and my siblings are the same. It's just what you do. I'll give you another example …

I'm driving down the road, and there's a lump in the road and it turns out to be my neighbour, who's collapsed and died. And there was no next of kin. And so I said to the coroner: "Well, I know his name. I know who he is. Can we bury him in the local church?" And they said: "Yes, but you have to adopt him before we can do that." So, I adopted a dead body just because it was important for me. For this poor man who came from [country] – funnily enough from the town where my parents and my grandparents came from – so he could have a decent burial in our church. I don't tell people that story. I didn't think "I'm gonna go be a good person and adopt this person so that he has …". I just did it, and I didn't think much about it.'

The presence of her kindness in this description is most noticeable in the absence of her thinking about being kind or what that means and then consciously acting in accordance with that. Here, her morality is not based on a conscious comparison with some ideal. Rather, she aligns her morality with her way of being; it becomes simply the natural way that she responds to daily events. In this example, P5 received her kindness as a granddaughter and a daughter, and she lives out her kindness as a cousin and a neighbour. In what she described, all these identities are in harmony with one another. Discovery of how these identities come together did not necessarily take a conscious effort.

A similarly harmonious process was described by P6. She explored her entrepreneurial and philanthropic ventures in three phases. This is how she described the first phase:

'The first time I stepped into entrepreneurship was … I really loved international travel and I saw an opportunity to publish a newsletter to get American families out being adventurous again, because it was after September 11th. I love experiential education, by seeing first hand, so I would say it was a hobby business. It was something while I was in transition as a mother ... I wanted to start something ... I think what it did for me was it got me out of the US and out into the world, and then I started branding myself as somebody who's internationally oriented and adventurous.'

In this description, we can identify elements of her multiple identities. Her moral identity is reflected in her desire to get American families out being adventurous again, based on her belief that their attitudes toward travel had changed since the tragedy of 9/11. Her personal identity is reflected in her love of international travel and experiential education. These are things she could experience alone, without having to experience a relationship with anyone. These loves are a personal hobby. They do not have any moral conviction associated with them. Finally, when she became a mother, this was the beginning of a very important relational identity for her, and her entrepreneurial activities co-existed with her transition to motherhood. When asked what was the most self-defining moment during that process, she said:

'I guess it was the first time I tried to create something that was my idea, built with my capabilities, to step into an opportunity that I saw that looked of interest to me, that I thought might be of interest to others.

It was not a successful business. It was not something I chose to continue, because I discovered that the niche I was targeting was just too tiny and I don't like pushing sales. So I quickly shifted, and that opened another door, which was to start working with international non-profits.'

Nevertheless, that experience remains meaningful for P6 because, as she went on to say:

'Really, for me, the goal was never to create a big business. I just wanted to try something, and

I didn't want to go back into traditional companies and work for bosses. I wanted flexibility, and I'm mission driven, so I wanted to explore if I could create something.

So, yeah, I think looking back at it, I don't think I felt this way then. But looking back at it now that you're asking me to, I guess that was probably the first time that I created something. And now I don't create businesses. I create networks. I catalyse people to work toward things. I don't create business entities. I convene and connect people, and so it is entrepreneurial, but it's not entrepreneurial in, maybe, the traditional definition of what entrepreneurship is.'

The first entrepreneurial venture that P6 engaged in was a for-profit business. She started it as a mother who wanted to become an entrepreneur out of her love of international adventure and moral concern for other American families experiencing fear as a consequence of 9/11. Whether or not the venture succeeded was not the most consequential factor in her experience. What mattered was that she tried to create something that was genuinely hers. When she said "the first time that I created something", the 'I' that she refers to contains a particular mixture of her moral, personal and relational identities. The content of this 'I' was later transformed.

Many interviewees show similar sentiments in their own reflections. During the early stages of their exploration, their successes in their entrepreneurial or philanthropic ventures helps them achieve the power of their own visions, establish their own credentials (perhaps independent of family wealth) and accumulate the financial independence and flexibility they needed to take care of their families and the people they care about. At that point, some people choose to settle into a domain that they feel passionate about and begin to crystallise their entrepreneurial and philanthropic effort into those areas where they can:

- serve as a catalyst to inspire others;
- make an irreversible difference;
- set up infrastructure to help others succeed;

- continue expanding their exploration into areas that will help them discover more of their inner capabilities.

For most of our interviewees, this process of recognising which path (or paths) are for them is a process that takes years, not months, to mature. For many, it is a journey that they still walk every day. P6 provided a depiction of this daily walk:

> 'I feel that I really deployed my best skills and really made a significant contribution in the non-profit in Africa that I worked with closely. I really helped them build significant parts of their business system. ... It was the second or third network that I got involved with, but with this one, I saw a huge gap where they had this beautiful vision to identify transformative youth on the continent of Africa and bring them together for an educational experience in America. And then, as I got closer and closer to it, I could see that they did such a great job identifying and developing these young people and that they were very successful [in] getting them into the United States.
>
> This is not me yet; this is building the background ... I could see that they were very successful in getting them into universities in the US and getting financial aid for them, but there it seemed to end. There were no staff over here in the US. There weren't support programmes or a plan.'

P6 is highly reflective on what she considers to be hers and what is not. She invested heavily in getting to know the people and organisation before she discovered the philanthropic contribution she could psychologically own.

> 'It was a secondary school, and they got people into university far away from their homes and their support networks. So, I mean, a theme for me is caring, and I'm very intuitive, and I just said, like: "These folks, you know, 60 of them are gonna arrive, but there's no support network, and they're

going to 50 different colleges all over the United States. It's going to be a huge identity crisis for them and just physically and financially and emotionally and culturally challenging."

So that's when I stepped in to just say: "Hey. How can we help you? You know we're over here, and you guys don't have the staff – and we do." I anticipated that there were going to be needs, and I think from that point forward, because we were here and we got to know them, we were well placed to meet those needs.

From then on, I'd say I would just keep noticing, from listening to the youth in the network, what they wanted, and the first thing they said they wanted was to get together with each other. So we would host them in November. It turns out they all have different school calendars and different geographies, but we could get them together for Thanksgiving. So we started hosting a gathering, and then [the non-profit] helped pay for travel so they could all get here. So we started convening them and getting them together, and then, you know, we just knew that people would need help with getting winter clothing or basic stuff like that. So we started a host family programme to try to match the individual students with families where they were located.

And then we launched a scheme to help our students eventually transition back to Africa. I worried for the students and their wellbeing, and I worried about the mission of this entity. This was not supposed to be the fast track to the African brain drain. Rather, this was about identifying Africa's entrepreneurs who wanted to return to the continent to run their projects and build ventures and solve community issues. So, it got really scary because after studying abroad for so long, they didn't then have a bridge back to Africa. And so, now, I get to the thing that I'm the most proud of and that is that [my partner] and I built a bridge back to the continent for these youth and we used our networks very successfully [to] get people to hire them.'

Although the trait of 'caring' has remained constant throughout her entrepreneurial and philanthropic ventures, who she cares for has shifted dramatically, and who she is while she is doing the caring has also shifted. The circle of her caring expanded from her own family (that is, from her experience as a new mother) to people who are similar to her (that is, other American families) to people who are less similar to her (that is, youth from a different continent).

We can also see how her psychological ownership developed in the young entrepreneurs project. She felt that the approach the organisation was adopting was attractive but described it originally as "not me". As she began to develop her engagement, she had a sense that the US operation she worked with the organisation to build was 'mine' and the bridge 'they' built for students returning to Africa was 'ours'. She has grown into owning her domain and its associated processes.

It is important to note that while these innovations made a difference for the young people involved, P6 created something that was simultaneously meaningful for her and the social reality of facilitating talented young entrepreneurs to return to the countries of their birth and make their own important contribution to their communities. As she transitioned from her earlier ventures to her later ones, her identities of being an internationally oriented, adventurous and caring person have all been clarified and obtained a much richer level of meaning through her encounters with people and how she chooses to work to serve them.

With both P5 and P6, through the caring and kindness they experienced from their nuclear families, be it the family that P5 grew up with or the family that P6 raises as a mother, they have found their own way of developing and expressing themselves in the wider circles of their philanthropy. For P7, his philanthropic experience reconnects him to the childhood identity that he developed through exposure to his grandfather's generosity. When asked what he got from his life that he would not have gotten had it not been for this philanthropic journey, P7 said:

'Had I not ventured into the not-for-profit world I would not have experienced the level of caring and interconnectedness I find there.

People in the not-for-profit world  care about others and social impact. They're giving and, excuse the expression, "charitable". The people in this world work hard and they get paid less, but there's a high level of devotion. This is evidenced in the work that we do [at EFE]. What we're doing there is way beyond anything I ever was able to create with my for-profit entities.'

As we can see from this description, P7 clearly identifies himself with one group of people, but not the other, and he uses the word 'we' to describe the group that he identifies with. He continued:

'We really knock the ball out of the park in many ways. That not only is reflected in terms of the non-profit work but how we relate to each [other], how we care about each other and how they care about me.

I was visiting one of our affiliates three years ago, and one of the rooms at the foundation office was locked. I was surprised and a little disappointed they wouldn't let me in the room. Later that afternoon, they opened the door and I discovered that they had been decorating the room for a surprise birthday party for me. They'd gone to a huge amount of effort.

As you can see,  we've created a logical family; we not only work together but we by and large like each other. In the for-profit world I came from that wasn't the norm. Quite frankly, I think I've got more out of my work at EFE than I put into it. It has really been a joy.'

Often. this kind of joy experienced from relationships is not planned. It is something that people encounter and then recognise as something that resonates with them. The contrast between their experience of the business community and their philanthropic community often helps them complete the cycle of dis-identifying themselves from one group of people ('this group is not me') and identifying themselves with another one ('this group is me').

P7 was asked whether having this experience came as a surprise rather than being something he set out to find, and he replied:

> I just didn't know. I assumed people are people. I didn't realise how diverse they could be and how people who choose to devote their lives to the non-profit world just have a different orientation, different compass.

For many, this is not an experience people can plan to have. They do not choose to enter philanthropy in a hunt to find a family in a group of hard-working and caring people. They are typically drawn to philanthropy to solve a problem, to make an impact or to do some *thing* or promote some *value* that is worthwhile. But what they often discover on that journey is connection, not only with other people but also a deeper sense of connection with who they truly are. Very often the root of who they are is planted early and then rediscovered or further developed through the experience of philanthropy. For P7, this root could be traced back to his experience with his grandfather.

> 'The richest person I've ever met in my life was my grandfather. He was wealthy beyond (imagining) yet he didn't have much money.
> To me, wealth is not what you have. It's a function of what you have versus what you think you need. My grandfather came over here from Poland at age 16 and worked hard to support his family and others.
> At the time of my birth, three generations of my family lived in a two-family house which meant that my grandfather was an integral and important part of my life. His determination to do the right thing, no matter the cost and regardless of what others thought of him is deeply imprinted in the core of my being. He brought over 42 people from Europe and saved their lives when things got dicey over there, which wasn't [an] easy thing for him to do, because the people he brought over were Orthodox Jews. He was not.
> They kind of looked down on him. They'd look him in the eye and say "you're a bad Jew", all because he

didn't observe all the customs that they did. He didn't keep kosher, he worked on the Shabbats, etc. But he brought them over and was very happy to do so, not needing anything in return.

He gave so much to so many, including to me; making my life a lot easier. So if I can attribute any influence in my life, it's probably him; it's his fault!'

When asked how he reconciles his childhood experience with his entrepreneurial experience and his philanthropic experience, he said: "My philanthropy is definitely more aligned with the value system that my grandfather exemplified; that was ingrained in me. He and I were very close. We spent a lot of time together and so I could see who he really was." This relates to P7's relational and moral identity. His close experience with his grandfather exposed him to philanthropy for the first time. He learned that his grandfather took steps to rescue those fleeing persecution in Europe. He saw what his grandfather did, but he also learned to reflect on why and how that spoke to the richness of who his grandfather was. In his second encounter with philanthropy, following a successful career in business, he remembers the kindness and unconditional support his grandfather had shown to others. He remembers his grandfather's morality and passion for acting in accordance with a personal code. This came to resonate with him as he found himself surrounded by others with a similar mindset – a new family, with its roots in the past, that allowed him to celebrate his identity as a deeply loving grandchild of someone who had meant so much.

## Conclusion

In this chapter, we introduced the concept of self and explained three types of self: moral identity; personal identity; and relational identity. Largely, moral identity is viewed as relational in nature. We used three illustrations to show that one's moral identity (for example, being a caring and kind person) can be developed early in life through one's relational identity in one's family (as we saw with P5 and P7). Moral identities initiated and nurtured during childhood can go on to develop more expanded meanings and expressions though one's business experiences and philanthropy (as we saw with P5, P6 and P7). Their impact can then come full circle, developing the very relational identities that first nurtured them, thereby providing additional and highly significant sources of meaning (as we saw with P6).

# 4

# Identity ceding

In all the examples we have shared so far, we have highlighted points in our interviewees' entrepreneurial or philanthropic journeys where their multiple identities can co-exist or change in harmony with one another while they serve the people they care about. Even when P7 feels that his moral identity is somewhat suffocated during his wealth accumulation journey, he is able to uphold the values of honesty and trustworthiness as a connection to a value system embedded in him through his grandfather.

Many of our interviewees, however, experience situations in which conflicts have to be overcome for them to succeed in their chosen journeys. Sometimes those conflicts are because of differences between their own goals, values and objectives and those of others. In other situations, conflict arises because the interviewees' sense of self is not in alignment with how others see them or who others need them to be. Sometimes these differences create a deep sense of conflict and the continuation or success of their philanthropy is contingent on this being resolved.

Navigating these difficulties is more difficult in some circumstances than in others. No philanthropic endeavour can exist in a vacuum, independent of the social realities in which it operates, whether that be the latest scandals associated with the effective altruism movement (MacAskill, 2016; Washburn, 2023), which provides the context for P1's philanthropy, our society's reliance on fossil fuels, where P4 grew his wealth, or the social justice systems that sometimes benefit and other times hurt our interviewees or the people they aim to support. The meaning of all philanthropy is ultimately drawn (at least in part) from the context in which it operates. It therefore follows that the creation of additional meaning from philanthropy can involve the changing of one or more of its associated social realities. Who we are in those social realities is critical. Philanthropic meaning can evolve from the exploration and morphing of our sense of self as we respond to each reality.

But we shouldn't over-claim here. There are a multitude of entrepreneurial or philanthropic engagements that do not need to align with our sense of who we are. Some decisions are simply low-involvement decisions that people do not take psychological ownership of. This is often the case when donations are small, the monies are used to support a long-standing programme (whose utility has already been proven) or one's sense of self is irrelevant to the nature of the gift (for example, financial support offered through a business' corporate social responsibility programme). In these low-involvement scenarios, it is rare for individuals to experience challenges in managing differences between them and the focal community in what they take ownership of or what they believe to be morally right.

The situation becomes more difficult when decisions are high involvement and when individuals experience psychological ownership of their goals, values and objectives to the degree that they become self-defining. In such circumstances, any difference with others or any disappointment they experience from their philanthropic efforts is not experienced merely as a difference in how people think, feel or believe. Rather, these are experienced as differences in the person's sense of who they are and who others are. If the level of difference is too great, it can make it difficult for individuals to come together and remain engaged.

Previous research as well as our interviews confirm that when navigating difference becomes too challenging, people can disengage from their psychological ownership (for example, 'this activity is no longer mine') or they may exit physically from the activity (Grimes, 2018). More subtle techniques that have also been found to help people navigate differences include reducing the importance of certain activities to the person's sense of who they are (for example, 'my philanthropy defines who I am, but my entrepreneurship does not'; Reed and Forehand, 2019), separating a sense of morality from certain issues (for example, 'whether I help this group of people is a personal preference, not a moral issue'; Skitka et al, 2021) and compartmentalisation (for example, 'this is what I do in my entrepreneurship or my philanthropy, but not how I live my identity as a father or mother'; Reed and Forehand, 2019). Because these strategies have already been widely studied in previous research, we do not expand on them here. Suffice it to say that prematurely curtailing what could otherwise be very meaningful philanthropic activities, both for the philanthropists and the communities they support, can result in significant waste and is something we hope this research can help reduce.

The psychological processes we explore in this chapter are most relevant to situations where the social reality individuals would like to create is deemed important to their essential sense of who they are but who they are in those situations, at least initially, does not quite gel with who they need to be to achieve their philanthropic goals. In these situations, people must make decisions about how much of themselves they are willing to allow others to shape in order to achieve a collective good.

The term 'willing' is important here because when people are willing to change, they seem to be able to persist in their philanthropic journey longer and experience a greater sense of wellbeing. We found that as people begin to navigate potentially conflict-inducing challenges, new and unexpected sources of meaning could emerge as they work toward a resolution. We found two mechanisms that seemed to us highly significant in this regard. Additional meaning could be created when:

- the individual's sense of self becomes more closely aligned with the people they want to help;
- the individual's sense of self becomes more closely aligned with their sense of who they truly are.

In this chapter, we focus on the first of these. We use P8 to illustrate how the mechanism works.

## Morphing identity: the case of P8

P8's first meaningful entrepreneurship venture was the business that he started 40 years ago and which became the focus of his career.

It was a startup that he took through the entire entrepreneurial process, from initial idea to execution to growth and, ultimately, to profitability. He also navigated it through several changes in ownership structure: going public; returning to private ownership; and, eventually, going public again.

He considers that this business taught him everything that he needed to learn about management, leadership, managing competition, creating a corporate culture that is attractive for people to come to and work in, providing a mission that is easily definable, drawing in talent, and attracting and retaining clients. P8 also created a series of other enterprises along the way, and, together, these activities, along with his upbringing and familial experience, have shaped his sense of who he is.

At the time of interview, he is 17 years into his philanthropic journey. As was the case with his entrepreneurial activities, his philanthropic activities have continued to shape his sense of who he is. Recalling how he started his philanthropic journey, he said:

> 'The original intention was actually a simple thing. The community believed in education and they wanted to send their kids to universities, but they couldn't afford it. So, for us, we wanted to establish a scholarship-granting organisation, but we wanted to have it associated with community work.
>
> So you get a scholarship, but you also agree to come and work in the community to help solve community problems. The idea here was not charity. We're not giving out scholarships; rather, we want to build character. We want to teach you things and engage with you in the community centre with things that you will not learn in your school or in your university so that once you go to the real world, you have that sense of community, that sense of problem-solving, that sense of initiative, which was missing because people felt that only the government provides.
>
> If the streets are dirty and the government is not cleaning the streets, we complain about the government, but they are our streets. If our houses are ruined, and we don't know how to fix them, they

are still our houses. If our neighbour is in need, he is still our neighbour. So how do we create volunteerism and do community work? So that's what we wanted to do originally. We wanted to keep our focus there and to do community work within that framework.'

P8's chosen domain is youth education, and his chosen process is provision of scholarships coupled with volunteerism. When P8 first began his philanthropic journey, he functioned using the self that he built from his early life, which comprised his personal entrepreneurial identity (of being able to leverage opportunities and succeed), his strong family relational identity and the collective identities he built through his friendships and business relationships. Figure 4.1 depicts P8's sense of self and the relationship he had with the community when he began his philanthropic activities.

What was shared between P8 and the community is a desire to provide young people with an education that they currently cannot afford. Also note that when asked why *he* started *his* philanthropy, P8 defines his philanthropic purpose by what the community he works with deems important. Note that he said: "the community believed in education", not 'I believed in education, and I think the community should too'. Although he shares the same purpose as the community, he does not take ownership of defining the purpose. He attributes ownership of that to the community.

What P8 does take ownership of, though, is the particular way that he chooses to provide this education – through a scholarship that requires volunteerism. He experiences a sense of moral conviction that this is the right approach. He does not want

**Figure 4.1:** P8's initial relationship with the community

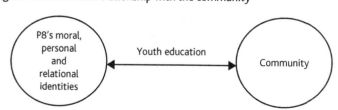

to practise handout philanthropy; rather, he wants to build the character of young people so as to equip them to step up and take care of their own communities.

Despite the clarity of purpose, because of the challenges posed by P8's social reality, it took longer than expected for his philanthropy to fulfil the designated purpose.

> 'We ended up, in the very early days, being overwhelmed because when you go to people in need, they will ask you for everything, because they don't have anything. They say: "We are jobless. We don't have bus stations. We don't have a post office. We don't have a clinic. We don't have a police station. Our kids are taking drugs in the streets." You tell them: "I want to help you." And they tell you: "Okay, you want to help me. Here's what my problems are." And we couldn't come into this community and act like consultants and say: "We will only do this, and we will only do that." I mean, that's bullying. And nobody will take you seriously. So, we were overwhelmed by what we were learning.'

For P8 the hardest part about overcoming this initial period of challenge was learning how to listen and using that listening to build trust. He went on to explain:

> 'When I first visited the community, I sat with their elders to tell them what I wanted to do. I was a complete alien. They lived 20 minutes away from my house, but I was still an alien to them. I could be in New York as far as they were concerned.'

The notion that, at the outset, he was "a complete alien" to the community elders is important. In psychological terms, he was perceived as a member of an 'outgroup', and consequently they did not trust him to have their best interests at heart (Sargeant and Lee, 2002). An identity barrier had been created, as depicted in Figure 4.2.

In order to break down the identity barrier, P8 shared the core of his approach.

**Figure 4.2:** The identity barrier that exists despite shared purpose

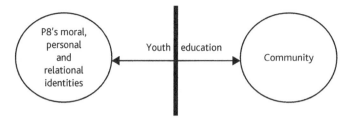

'The first decision we took was that I made sure that our operations and offices would be in the community. Our first director was saying: "Okay, let's have an office somewhere else, and we only come in the morning for the job and go." I said: "No, you live in the community. They have to see you every single day. You have to live with them. You have to eat with them. You have to see their streets at all times, and nothing happens outside of the community."'

He also sought to build trust by addressing various community needs.

'They [the community] asked for one school. We fixed five.
  They asked for a clinic. We built a clinic.
  They asked for a police station. We lobbied government to get them a police station.
  They asked for a post office. We got them a post office.
  And then, *over and above*, we had our community centre.'

It is important to note that what was originally the single essential goal for P8 (that is, creating a community centre) became subordinated to community needs. His dream of a community centre was later positioned as "*over and above*" what the community regarded as the essentials. The purity and strength of P8's moral convictions are reflected in his decision to serve what the community deemed significant before what he deemed significant (Skitka et al, 2021). But what he yielded to the community is much more than his philanthropic priorities. He also yielded part of his sense of who he is to the community.

## Defining identity ceding

We define *identity ceding* as a psychological process in which people willingly allow their *sense of self* to be transformed in order to achieve the goals they share with a community.

It is a process that often takes years to come to fruition. P8 was so deeply convinced that his shared goal with the community was the right thing for him personally and was deemed significant by the community, he was willing to morph his sense of who he was (that is, a "king" in his own organisation) to achieve this goal.

Identity transformation is not something that emerges through simple agreement over a shared sense of purpose. Instead, it is the transformation, on an ongoing basis over a long period of time, of how people act, think and feel. Over the 17 years that P8 has been working with this community, he has gradually become part of the community, physically, psychologically and socially.

> 'I was there practically every weekend, and so I got to understand what it is and how it works and be part of it. That's how I understood all these challenges. There is a sense of humility there, because in your organisation you are king, yet here you are completely in a mindset that requires extreme sensitivity.'

We found that five types of self can be involved in identity ceding: the agentic self; the object self; the experiential self; the represented self; and the meta-self. We explore the first four of these in pairs:

- the agentic self (I) versus the object self (me);
- the experiential self versus the represented self

### Agentic self versus object self

The agentic self is the 'I' who evaluates the options of the selves available to the individual and can choose to cede aspects of their object self (in P8's case, the king) to what the community needs them to become (in P8's case, a sensitive listener) in order to achieve shared goals. Identity ceding primarily describes a process engaged in by the agentic self, which has the capacity to change what the object self is. In P8's example, his agentic self changes his object self from a king to a sensitive listener. He finds that although the loss of his king identity could be perceived as a negative, the gain of his sensitive listener self more than compensates for that. By ceding P8's object self (his king identity), he is able to adopt and develop his sensitive listener identity. This gain has rather a profound impact on his life. P8 explained:

'I benefited from that [humility] in my organisation, and there is a mutual benefit in all this.'

'[My philanthropic experience] shaped me because it got me to understand communities. Really, [my philanthropy] taught me a big lesson.'

When the sensitivity obtained from one aspect of a person's life (in P8's case, philanthropy) benefits another aspect (in P8's case, his business), we know a transformation has occurred in their holistic way of being and is not just about how they behave in a particular compartment of their life.

Similarly, when what is being transferred is not just isolated knowledge (for example, how to build trust with a focal community), but a generalisable pattern of behaviour (for example, sensitivity in listening), the transformation takes place at the level of the person's sense of self and is not just about what their selves know or how the selves behave in isolated situations. The transformation involves both:

- the object self (me) being transformed (for example, from a king to a sensitive listener);
- the agentic self (I) being willing to engage in such a transformation process.

While our interviewees are often aware of the transformation that occurs in their object self, very rarely do they reflect on their agentic self and the role it might play in a process of transformation. That is, they may recognise, in the same way as P8, that their object self has transformed, but still be unaware of the agentic self or the fact that it is taking decisions and instigating behaviours associated with the transition.

These decisions of the agentic self are about choosing which identity to live by and are often made on a moment-by-moment basis. This is especially hard in the early stages of a transformation journey, because people are still much more used to living in the default mode of who they are (for example, a king) than in a new mode (for example, a sensitive listener). Often, the same choice has to be made repeatedly for a long period of time before an identity transformation can be achieved.

Without reflection about the object and the agentic self, however, our interviewees are often not aware of the extent to which their thoughts, feelings and behaviours are routinised as the object self way of being. It takes a lot of practice and monitoring for their agentic self to reset the pattern and gradually take hold and permeate their thoughts, feelings and behaviour patterns. It is not something that can happen overnight.

### Experiential self versus represented self

To complicate things further, when the agentic self is making a decision about which identity to cede and how, it often experiences this process without necessarily representing what it is experiencing (Legrand and Ruby, 2009). That is, when the agentic self is making momentary decisions about whether one should live like, say, a king or a sensitive listener, it does not simultaneously monitor who is making this decision. It could be the king, the sensitive listener or, indeed, another represented self making this decision.

In other words, people can form a representation about who their agentic self (I) is, or they can experience the agentic self as an experiential self without forming any mental representations of it. One's agentic self can simply be an experience that happens. People can decide *like* a king or *like* a sensitive listener without necessarily representing themselves as either. Indeed, most of the time when we asked our interviewees who is making the decision

**Table 4.1:** The four selves involved in identity ceding

| Experiential/ Represented selves | Agentic self | Object self |
|---|---|---|
| Experiential selves: king versus listener | I make this decision like a king or like a sensitive listener, but I do not represent myself in either of these ways. I am willing to make decisions like a sensitive listener more than a king, but I do not represent myself in either of these ways. (Identity ceding) | |
| Represented selves: king versus listener | I know it is the king in me who is making this decision. | I am a king. |
| | I know it is the sensitive listener in me who is making this decision. | I am a sensitive listener. |
| | I choose the sensitive listener in me, over the king, to make this decision. (Identity ceding) | I am either a king or a listener. |

and how they characterise the person who is making the decision, they could not say more than 'I am'. They could not articulate their sense of self beyond it is 'who I am'. This is the case even if they are consciously aware that they are, say, a king or a sensitive listener in their object self (me). That is who they are. They just could not point to the representation that is taking agentic actions or find it possible to label them as such.

By definition, an object self cannot be an experiential self, because it is a representation that people have about who they are – it is not the agentic 'I', who acts. Hence the separation noted in Table 4.1.

It is important to recognise the intricacies of how these different types of self become part of the identity ceding process. This is because until a person makes more and more decisions in the manner of, say, a sensitive listener, they do not necessarily know that they have a sensitive listener identity and hence they cannot choose to function as such.

It is only after they have established a rather consistent pattern of thinking, feeling and doing things *like* a sensitive listener that they become aware of and represent their own sense of self in this identity. Actions taken before they reach this level of awareness are merely reflective of the nature of a sensitive listener. These are actions that P8's agentic self experienced and which formed the building blocks of who he was becoming (that is, more like a sensitive listener). Often, this kind of identity formation process takes an extended period of time. In P8's case, it was a process lasting almost 20 years.

Most often, these identity transformations are not detectable through introspection, because they have yet to be formulated into mental representations that are detectable. People may make a momentary decision which is different from what would result from their default king mode, but they do not yet have a new identity with which to associate that experience. When these unaligned experiences happen often enough and leave a strong enough impression, people become aware of the patterns and form a representation to host and collate them into a new sensitive listener identity. The crucial building blocks of those momentary ceding experiences go largely unnoticed, yet without them identity ceding can never happen, and the new sensitive listener identity can never be formed.

This may suggest that in order to deepen or sustain their philanthropic experience, HNWIs and UHNWIs should volunteer more often with the people they care about. In this way, people can have more opportunities to experience identity ceding. But volunteering alone, without a willingness to morph one's self for the fulfilment of a purpose shared with an individual or a community, is not necessarily going to transform the king to a sensitive listener or create more community good. So how do we capture the precise directionality of identity ceding and help facilitate it to create more meaningful philanthropy?

## Directionality and identity ceding

The choices our agentic self makes are at the heart of identity ceding. The agentic self can choose to advance a shared purpose as its default approach without any willingness to morph identity. Alternatively, the agentic self can choose to morph its own sense of who it is in order to fulfil a shared purpose. In the latter case, it puts the achievement of the shared purpose before the maintenance of its own sense of who it already is. Its sense of self is then transformed as it fulfils the shared purpose.

In contrast to other approaches suggested to philanthropists, the unique directionality inherent in identity ceding presents a rather unique way for individuals to practise their philanthropy. Enlightened philanthropists have long been willing to morph what they want to do for a community to fit better with the needs the community itself feels it has. But by being open to identity ceding, the philanthropist is also willing to morph their sense of who they are in order to become who the community needs them to be.

It is important to note, though, that identity ceding does not necessarily lead to the recommendation that people with resources must be willing to relinquish their control over what they deem to be important in a philanthropic situation. Where identity ceding takes place, such decisions will eventually be made jointly by a newly formed collective. It is in the interest of both parties that all resources that can contribute to the collective good be effectively marshalled. That may require the philanthropist to act as who they are in other contexts (for example, a powerful lobbyist of government) to benefit the focal community, rather than acting always as the community per se. Identity ceding does not imply subservience, but rather a directional intent to serve the community not only through what they do but also through who they are.

## Creation of a new social reality

It is important to recognise that identity ceding does not occur in a vacuum. It occurs in a social reality, and it has the potential to create a new social reality. This is how P8 described the new social reality created through his identity ceding process. Describing his experience of becoming a part of the community, he said:

> 'After 17 years of living in a community, you get to understand each other very well, and you get to know what you can and what you cannot do, what our capabilities are. We're now just part of them.

The communities we operate in, for instance, they are religious, and we are a secular organisation. And so there were some who lobbied against us because we got girls and boys to meet in the same room.

We wanted to break those barriers, but we didn't come and say: "Well, here's what we're gonna do." We can't force it on them. But slowly, and once they trusted us, they knew that their girls were safe in the community centre. So, if they're with us, then they're with family.'

In time, P8, his community centre and the broader community have become a family (see Figure 4.3). The change in his identity from being an "alien" to being a family member is endorsed by the community. In his ceding of his king identity, he and the community, together, are creating a new social reality, a familial one that does not treat him as an outgroup member or as alien. Whatever change is created by this family is now regarded as a change in *their* lives through *their* efforts.

It should be noted that the creation of this new shared familial social reality, built through trust, does not require either P8 or the community to give up all meaningful differences between them. The continuation of some difference is important for P8.

'We work with them on all of these things. It's not as if we parachute in from outside. We basically engage them

**Figure 4.3:** Development of a new social reality

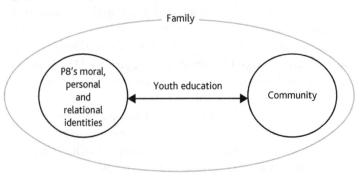

to be part of the solution, but because we are who we are and we had access, we were able to do things that they couldn't. It's not only about money. It's about the ability to lobby [the] government to get things done.'

Note the expression "because we are who we are". P8 does not attempt to become similar to the community he serves in all respects, because if that had happened, he would have lost his ability to make a difference for them and with them. Instead, he makes good use of the differences between himself and the community (for example, when using his ability to lobby the government and thus create a collective good).

His identity ceding process builds trust through promise fulfilment on issues that mattered to the community and were outside of his original intent (McBride, 2022; McBride and Wuebker, 2022). In this way, he creates a more trusting family-like social reality and breaks down the identity wall through his identity transformation (that is, from 'my' versus 'their' family members to 'our' family members).

It should be noted too that for his original intent to be fulfilled, he does not have to break down the outgroup wall completely with regard to all parties. There will always be people who protest what he does from within the community. Equally, he does not have to build 100 schools or 400 clinics to achieve a change. P8 and the community reach a mutual understanding about what could be done and what could not. Proper boundaries are set, but these boundaries are familial ones for the advancement of the shared purpose.

## The role of trust

The theme of trust pervaded much of our interviews, and this is deemed by many of our interviewees to be one of the most crucial, if not the most crucial, ingredient. So we explored whether the trust P8 built through his philanthropy is different from the trust built in his entrepreneurship activities. His answer was:

'Partially, yes. I mean, in the very early days, maybe, there is some similarity. When you're building a new business, you work very hard to establish your credentials as a founder, as a CEO, as somebody that is going out to serve a certain challenge and create a business out of it. So, when you're recruiting people, obviously, you have to convince people that there is a future here. This is a very young organisation, and people have a preference to work for big organisations. I'm talking about the 1980s, so this was before the sexiness of startups, right? So, you have to work very hard to convince people that they have a future. So, there is that trust process, and you only prove it by action, by doing things, by them experiencing the environment and the work. They need to feel that they're contributing and benefiting and they are generating their own knowledge and their own wealth.

When you go to communities that live on the margins … I felt it very clearly when we wanted to establish our first community centre in one of the marginalised communities. This was much more than recruiting people for a job. They are extremely protective, and it took them a while to trust.

We addressed that very quickly by asking them for certain things that they wanted the community to have, even though it was not part of our original mission [for example, the schools, clinics, post office and police station]. And we went out and did everything they asked for, so they can then trust that we talk and we execute and we deliver on our promises.

Theoretically and practically, it is the same. People will trust you as a leader, or as somebody that wants to do things, when they see you in action and delivering on your promise. That is a rule that will never change.

The difference is that in my business, I can say: "Here's how we operate, and anybody that works with us has to operate within that." People have to be aligned very quickly. You act much more forcefully as a leader in a business. In philanthropy, you have to be much more sensitive to the community because it's theirs. Even after a while, the community is the community, and you need to operate within it.'

The essence of the moral values that P8 embraces as his own have not changed across his entrepreneurial and philanthropic activities. He needs to be trustworthy, which is one of the most common traits that people use to describe their moral identity (Aquino and Reed, 2002). However, what this moral value means differs based on the context – his entrepreneurial versus his philanthropic activities.

In his business, trust is built by remaining true to the alignment he is clear he wants to create. As staff and other stakeholders see this applied in his decision making and the environment he begins to create, trust is developed.

In his philanthropy, trust is built by allowing the focus of that alignment to be changed. As he cedes something of himself to become part of the community, the notion of any separation between his goals, values and objectives and those of the community ceases to have meaning. Trust is now built not by delivering on 'his' promises, but on 'our' promises.

Traditionally, we may think of becoming part of the community as shrinking the psychological distance experienced between us and the community or increasing the degree to which our self overlaps with the essence of the community (Aron et al, 1992). In Figures 4.1–4.3, rather than depicting two circles far apart from one another, we might thus depict two circles moving gradually closer to one another or even overlapping. That developing closeness is experienced by P8 and many of our interviewees in their philanthropy (Sternberg, 1986).

However, as we have seen, for P8 and many of our other interviewees to succeed, some difference has to be maintained between them and their focal communities. Indeed, being realistic about what is changeable and pragmatic about how to drive change are common traits among our interviewees.

We used P8's life and his entrepreneurial and philanthropic journeys to illustrate how identity ceding works and how four types of selves may be involved in the identity ceding process. P8 had a holistic upbringing and now manages his philanthropy by applying his knowledge and experience of being a family member, a friend and a successful business leader. In most of what P8 shared, he was functioning in what many would consider non-abusive or non-traumatic situations. His philanthropic experience did not trigger any uncomfortable reactions from his past. By and large, he has also succeeded in achieving his philanthropic objectives in a secular way, without drawing on any spiritual beliefs, resources or insights.

Not all identity ceding shared by our interviewees exhibits the same characteristics. Next, we explore how identity ceding can be experienced in two very different scenarios: when one's philanthropic experience becomes a trauma trigger (P6); and when people engage a religious or spiritual identity to remain true to their philanthropic intent (P9).

### Identity ceding and trauma: the case of P6

P6 grew up in an abusive family environment, and severe childhood trauma left a deep imprint on her. Having accumulated the wealth necessary to practise philanthropy, she supports others not only with money but also by donating her time to a mentorship programme. During what are often long-term (for her) mentorship relationships, she can experience identity ceding as an ongoing struggle of the agentic self, choosing to cede her object identity as a childhood trauma survivor to the object identity of a "regenerative adult" (her words) so that she can best support her mentees.

P6 shared that through years of counselling related to her childhood experience, she has gained rather sophisticated self-reflection skills that allow her to monitor not only her object selves (that is, childhood trauma survivor or regenerative adult) but her agentic self, who needs to choose between the object selves. Her agentic self often recognises when she functions out of her childhood trauma survivor identity and when she functions out of her regenerative adult identity.

To illustrate the relevance of this identity-shifting process, P6 shared a situation where she provided mentoring support for one of her mentees while the mentee was experiencing a significant personal crisis. P6 had had a relationship with the mentee for over ten years. P6 had to turn down a request for crisis funding from this mentee about six months before our interview, and the mentee reconnected about one month before our interview with some devastating news. The mentee's marriage had ended and her business with her ex-husband had fallen apart.

The crisis situation shared by the mentee triggered trauma for P6. Her agentic self was aware that her childhood trauma survivor identity was pressing to take over from her regenerative adult self and thus prevent her from giving her mentee the best support she could offer. This is how she explained the situation:

'About a week ago, she [the mentee] came back and sent me this incredibly long email, like ten paragraphs, that made her sound literally unwell. She's really not well. She's a mathematician, but very in touch with emotions and stuff. She really was in a crisis.

But it was triggering me. So this is one of these situations where my inner child was getting triggered and the generative, wanting to be a helpful woman, is showing up too, and then the ebb and flow [what we would call the agentic self] is dealing with the conflict between the two.

So I started processing myself what I would be willing to offer her. Because this is where the inner child conflicts with what's really possible for a person like me [the adult regenerative self], who lives far away and is not a family member. And my foundation was not geared, nor my life geared, to go in and rescue individuals in crisis. However, she's one of my closer mentees. So it triggered [me] a lot.

She and I got emails back and forth, and I said: "I have to be honest with you. I'm so scared about [your experience] and this is triggering a lot for me personally given my childhood."

I reminded her that this is triggering my early belief that I grew up with, that I have to rescue people and that I have to save people, and I said: "I know that's not the case and now, as an adult, I know I can't fix your life. I can't rescue you but I am willing to offer you some assistance in some specific ways, and so let me think about that and get back to you." So I offered her four possibilities of ways I could help her.'

Here, P6's agentic self chooses to cede her childhood trauma survivor identity to her adult regenerative self, to support her mentee through the latter identity. The demands of her trauma survivor identity remain, but are ceded to the regenerative adult and thus P6 'speaks' through the latter's voice. While her child defaults to the need to help everyone in pain, her regenerative adult understands that to protect P6, and for her help to be meaningful, boundaries must be placed on that support.

Nevertheless, her regenerative adult self recognises that it can allow itself to accept additional behaviours and grow the relationship with the mentee as a consequence. She shared: "I'm more able to share my vulnerability, more able to set boundaries but explain why ... and that sharing has brought us a lot closer." Through sharing her experience of being both triggered by trauma and able to cede her childhood trauma survivor identity to her adult regenerative identity, she finds a way to support her mentee, increasing intimacy while at the same time identifying and applying new boundaries.

Anybody who has obtained psychological counselling to cope with social situations may reach P6's level of self-awareness. In her philanthropy journey, however, P6 chooses to use that self-awareness to serve a mentee. She chooses to go there and experience the ceding, because she cares:

> 'Anyway, I feel for me [her agentic self] some of these decisions are really hard, and I'm sure they feel that way, because those who've turned to philanthropy probably have more empathy and they really are using that same empathy to make a difference in society.
>
> So, of course, the more you see how hard it is to actually transform a life ... it's probably much harder work than selling a product or developing and selling a product. That's hard work too because you're creating something that didn't exist. But to actually get a youth out of poverty or to get an adult on a functioning path when they've faced so many barriers is really hard.

It's dependent on so many things that if you're an entrepreneur and you can just focus on one little thing, you can get a product off the ground. But to all of a sudden step into the bigger picture of how you really create change for people that is meaningful, sustainable and transformative is really hard. It's not easy at all.'

Very often, the philanthropist's agentic self simply makes these hard identity choices as experiential selves. That is, the person does not take the time to specify for themselves which self is acting – in P6's case, she could choose between the childhood trauma survivor and the regenerative adult. In doing so, we think, they are wasting an opportunity to make their philanthropy more meaningful and sustainable.

## The meta-self

We think P6 becoming aware of the fact that her agentic self is at work and then making really hard decisions is important. Without this awareness, she would not be able to begin to build the skills she needs to care for her agentic self and create conditions in which the hard decisions can become easier to make. The fifth type of self, the meta-self, is relevant during these processes (Shang, 2019).

The meta-self has been widely studied in the field of psychology (Bahl and Milne, 2010). It is the self that consciously manages the conflicts between two or more agentic selves, who may be in competition with each other for resources, such as attention, mental processing capacities or actions (Hermans et al, 1992; Bahl and Milne, 2010). While the agentic selves make decisions about the object selves, the meta-self makes decisions about the agentic selves. It includes multiple agentic selves, the object selves they manage, the understanding that agentic selves can be in conflict with each other and the momentary hierarchies of these selves. In the context of identity ceding, the most relevant functions performed by the meta-self are:

• reinforcing the experiential agentic self to make the right decisions for the attainment of shared goals;

- forming a representation of an experiential agentic self who is making tough identity ceding decisions;
- reinforcing the represented agentic self whenever helpful for the attainment of shared goals.

An illustration is provided in Table 4.2. Here, P6's experiential agentic self is making many decisions like a regenerative adult. Her meta-self can increase her willingness to make more decisions in this manner as a way of reinforcing this experiential agentic self without forming a representation of it.

P6's meta-self can also become aware that even though her experiential agentic self is making all these regenerative adult-like decisions, she does not think that her regenerative adult is

**Table 4.2:** Selves involved in identity ceding: the case of P6

| Role of the meta-self | Experiential/ Represented selves | Agentic self | Object self |
|---|---|---|---|
| Grow the willingness of the experiential 'I' to make decisions more like a regenerative adult, as the benefits of so doing are recognised. | Experiential selves: regenerative adult versus childhood trauma survivor | I am willing to make decisions more like a regenerative adult than a childhood trauma survivor, but I do not represent myself in either of these ways. (Identity ceding) | |
| Form a represented agentic self to increase its use in the future. | Represented selves: regenerative adult versus childhood trauma survivor | I know it is the child victim in me who is making this decision. | I am a child victim. |
| | | I know it is the regenerative adult in me who is making this decision. | I am a regenerative adult. |
| | | I choose the regenerative adult in me over the child victim to make this decision. (Identity ceding) | I am either a child victim or a regenerative adult. |

necessarily the represented self making these decisions. Hence, P6 does not represent herself as a regenerative adult and credit herself for being this kind of person when she makes adult-like decisions. To facilitate identity ceding, P6's meta-self can proactively form a representation of P6's experiential agentic self and provide her with verbal or mental reinforcement every time she decides as a regenerative adult.

For example, after P6 makes a decision as a regenerative adult, her meta-self can form the thought that this decision is made by a regenerative adult and the decision is good. It can also form the thought that the same regenerative adult can be engaged more readily in future decisions. As a result of this, P6's meta-self can help speed up the process through which her childhood trauma survivor identity can be ceded to her regenerative adult identity when it comes to making her philanthropic decisions. This function that the meta-self plays can obviously spill over from her philanthropic domain to influence other life decisions.

Unlike P8's king identity, which continues to be ceded, P6's childhood trauma survivor identity will likely be part of her sense of self for the rest of her life, no matter how many times her agentic self has practised ceding it to her adult regenerative self. It may simply be an ongoing battle that she has to fight. And unlike P8's sensitive listener identity, P6's regenerative adult identity is not inherently other-related or communal. Without ceding her childhood trauma survivor identity to her regenerative adult identity, however, P6 could not sustain her philanthropy in the way that led her to the quality philanthropic experience she has had. What matters in identity ceding is not necessarily that we cede our personal identities to the collective of a community, but that we are willing to morph our identities in ways that may be helpful to a community.

Another way to look at the same process reveals the benefit that identity ceding can accrue for the philanthropist. Without her philanthropy, P6 would never have recognised the quality of her regenerative adult self or what it can help others achieve. We think this is where people can obtain additional meaning from their philanthropy. Meaning is obtained through their engagement of their meta-self to facilitate the transformation of their agentic selves for a shared purpose. P6's mentee may only be one example from the community she cares for. Yet the same identity ceding process can benefit many others.

This kind of meaning may not be relevant to all. P8's identity ceding process, for example, may not involve high-intensity trauma triggers. It may require only his agentic self to cede identity. We do not think the meta-self is a necessary component in all identity ceding experiences. But in the circumstances where it is relevant, it can provide an additional source of meaning in philanthropy. Next, we use P9's experience to illustrate another situation in which the meta-self may become relevant.

### Faith, identity and the meta self: the case of P9

P9's challenge in philanthropy lies in the reality that he does not have enough resources to help all he feels compassion for and wants to help. How might he use identity ceding to allow him to sustain his philanthropy?

> 'If the giving that I was doing just came from me, then I have a finite limit to how much I can give. But if I feel I'm just the channel and I can access a divine source of love and it's infinite, you can really plug into that. Then you can give a lot more exponentially, more than you would if you were running just on your own juice.'

At any moment when a philanthropic opportunity arises, P9's agentic self can choose between running on his own batteries (that is, through his finite human being identity) or running on an infinite divine source (that is, through his human channel identity).

P9 defines himself as a channel, clarifying that he does not mean that he does not experience compassion for others when they suffer. Neither does he mean that he does not receive God's love himself. On the contrary, he believes that the divine source of love that he experiences allows him to feel exponentially more compassion toward others. His sustainability as a philanthropist does not lie in his ability to numb himself from experiencing compassion, withdraw from emotionally draining activities or compartmentalise the disappointment of being able to help only in some situations. Instead, he has found a way to practise his faith that sustains him within these constraints.

'When you see something that [would be] right and it doesn't happen, because you care, there is always obviously some kind of disappointment. I don't think that will ever change. But it doesn't mean that you don't have faith or that you cannot tap into [that faith] when the next opportunity arises.'

For P9, the degree to which one can tap into infinite love is not contingent on what he can or cannot achieve in any given situation, but whether his agentic self can cede his limited human identity to his human channel identity next time around, despite any prior disappointment.

As shown in Table 4.3, P9's experiential agentic self can experience every disappointment as a defeat of his limited human identity or a defeat of his channel identity. When the 'defeat' is experienced in the former way, this identity focuses his attention on a sense of limitedness and reduces the likelihood he will help in the future. But when it is experienced in the latter way, by a channel for divine love, it gives him hope and reassurance that there are other ways in which the person may be helped and that what he did do matters in some way. These thoughts encourage him to do more the next time when something is asked of him. For him to sustain his philanthropy, his experiential agentic self needs to become more willing to make decisions as a channel for the divine. Identity ceding can be experienced by his represented agentic self in a similar way.

Various faith- and non-faith-based spiritual traditions have different names for the infinite source of love that P9 described. Still, not everyone requires access to the divine in order to sustain their philanthropy. In the absence of faith, our interviewees are able to draw similar sustenance from a sense of community that is meaningful for them.

All our interviewees have experienced occasional losses or discouragement in their philanthropy. Indeed, some experienced repeated 'defeats'. But our interviews suggest that if one can continue to increase one's precision and persistence in choosing

**Table 4.3:** Selves involved in identity ceding: the case of P9

| Role of the meta-self | Experiential/Represented selves | Agentic self | Object self |
|---|---|---|---|
| Guide the 'I' to make decisions more like a channel for divine love once it assigns the right meaning to one's compassion and action, regardless of the observable outcomes they generate. | Experiential selves: finite human being versus a channel to divine love | I am willing to make decisions more like a channel for divine love than a finite human being. (Identity ceding) | I am a finite human being. |
| Translate an experiential agentic self into a represented agentic self and assign it the most sustainable meaning for your philanthropy, so it will be more likely chosen in the future. | Represented selves: finite human being versus a channel to divine love | I know it is the finite human being in me who is feeling disappointed. | I am a finite human being. |
| | | I know it is the channel to a divine source of love in me who is feeling disappointed. | I am a human channel to a source of divine love. |
| | | I choose to be a human channel to divine love when making my next philanthropic decision. (Identity ceding) | I am either a finite human being or a human channel to a source of divine love. |

the most sustainable form of represented agentic self to face these challenges, it is possible to continue to experience enriched meaning and thereby sustain one's philanthropy. These insights of how to fine-tune one's agentic self in order to sustain one's philanthropy are part of the content of the meta-self. The development of such insight in one's meta-self can, in and of itself, become a source of meaning for one's philanthropy. Such meaning can be delivered whether or not the philanthropy is 'successful'. The road map of how they experience meaning and how they sustain their philanthropy will simply look different.

As an example, many interviewees choose to do only what is sustainable within their financial, social and emotional resources, choosing not to worry about anything that is beyond their reach. In this way, they are less likely to experience disappointments in their philanthropy. At the same time, though, they are less likely to push the boundaries of what is humanly possible. For these individuals, doing what is possible is enough, and the strategy is sustainable because philanthropic victories are often observable and can be deeply meaningful. Yet the same strategy may not be sustainable for others, because pushing themselves beyond what is humanly possible is, for them, the deepest source of meaning that philanthropy can supply. Failure is evidence of 'striving to conquer' which is itself seen as meaningful and thus embraced as a gain, not a loss.

By specifying these different pathways, we are laying the groundwork to explain how different pathways for meaning can develop. We develop this line of thinking in much greater detail in our remaining chapters.

## Conclusion

In this chapter, we used P8's experience with his community centre to explain what identity ceding is. We explained the four types of self that can be involved in the identity ceding process. We explored why identity ceding can be an effective way to help people succeed in reaching their shared purpose with the communities they care about. We then used the example of P6 to show why gaining skills to monitor and reinforce one's identity ceding process can be beneficial not only to the individual themselves, but also to the people they intend to help through their philanthropy.

We also introduced a fifth type of self that could be involved in this process: the meta-self. We used the example of P9 to show how identity ceding can be used to help sustain people's philanthropic journey even in the case of ongoing defeats, and to show the role that the meta-self might play there. All of these examples together can help philanthropists discover a way to develop their sense of self in their philanthropy. In the next chapter, we explore how identity ceding can also help people align more closely with their sense of who they truly are, as well as to the community they intend to help.

# 5

# The essential self

In the previous chapter, we outlined a process through which people can cede their identities to achieve goals they share with a community. In so doing, they can sometimes create a social reality capable of delivering greater collective good than might otherwise have been possible.

We noted that at no point did any of our interviewees describe this identity ceding process as sacrificial or involve the giving up of oneself. Rather, it was perceived as developmental and enriching. We also described the potential benefit that identity ceding can deliver for philanthropists working in challenging circumstances using the examples of personal trauma (P6) and challenging social circumstances (P9).

Another benefit that this identity ceding process could deliver for our interviewees was the opportunity to discover, experience and express their essential self. The more closely the identities people need to cede are aligned with their sense of who they believe they are in essence, the more challenging the identity ceding process can become. However, the more people have clarity and conviction about who their essential self is, the more they are driven to discover the best way to manage their identity ceding process such that their essential self can be morphed into one through which the most collective good can be created. Next, we define what the essential self is and illustrate its properties.

## Defining the essential self

Psychologists describe what we consider to be the essence of ourselves using terms such as 'essential self', 'true self' and 'authentic self' (Strohminger et al, 2017). They believe that people have the ability to know who they truly are, were born to be or are meant to be. Extant research has shown that people have a tendency to behave in ways that are guided by their knowledge of their essential self (Schlegel et al, 2013). This research has also shown that across cultures, people believe that their essential self is morally good (Kim et al, 2022). What is considered morally good, however, differs based on culture and the social categories that people belong to (Newman et al, 2014). It is a concept people shape through their upbringing and the social realities they live in.

In our research, we identified several distinctive characteristics of the essential self that are new to the literature. Firstly, we found that our interviewees embrace a sense of the unknown in the essence of who they are. They accept it as something that they can continue to discover, experience and express. They are also comfortable allowing the unknown to guide their behaviour in the same way the known does.

Secondly, because of this open-mindedness regarding their own essence, they are also willing to shape their behaviour based on what they *believe* to be true about themselves, not just what they *know* to be true about themselves. They sometimes use their philanthropic activities as tools to explore and clarify what might comprise that essence.

Thirdly, a journey of exploration and clarification about their *singular* essential self typically becomes a journey of exploration and clarification about an essential self that is *collective* in nature. Very often, they achieve this understanding of their collective essence by searching for an alignment between what they see themselves as being born to be and what the community believes they need to be, in order for them to achieve a shared purpose. Interviewees often go through an essential self-realisation process to allow them to experience the strongest sense of fit with who they need to be to achieve shared purpose with the community. We use P10's experience to illustrate this process.

## Exploring the essential self: the case of P10

When asked what was the most meaningful of all the philanthropic activities he had undertaken to date, P10 said: "The most important one was actually the first one, where we supported a project in [country]. ... We went there in 1997. It basically set the way forward to what we are doing today."

This event occurred after P10's first 'cashing in' event, so he had the wealth necessary to practise philanthropy, as well as the time. P10 has always had a strong interest in nature, and "with a bit of time and money," he said, "we shopped around for a while, asked various charities for what they could suggest [in this field], and one of them came up with what sounded like a suitable idea." As a result, they went on this trip.

When asked about the moment that he knew this was the right project for him, P10 replied: "I've always been someone who likes nature." Then, when asked why he chose that particular project, he explained:

'That happened to be [country]. And, if you go there, you will know. When it started, I thought it was a conservation project and I'd pay money to protect animals and put up protective fences or whatever you do. So, when we travelled down there the first time, I thought it was to have a look at wildlife. But what I came away with was a completely overwhelming people experience.

It was what these people said and what they showed me, the way they viewed life. So, one example, we're talking to local people about trees and shrubs and I asked: "What's the use of this shrub?" They said: "We use the leaves, and we dry them, and we make tea. And that tastes good." "And what's the other one?" "We make some concoction that can cure your back, so these are good trees. They are usable trees." "And what about this tree?" "No, we can't do anything with it." And I say: "So, it's not a useful tree." "No, no, it's very useful, because the birds come to sit in it." So, that type of philosophy.

It gave me an insight and showed the way forward. It said, if I'm interested in nature conservation, these experiences told me that these people know what they're doing. They are already very good custodians of their own environment. So, why come down and tell them to do anything in a different way? Better to just support them.'

What P10 hears from the local people was more than what could or could not be done. He learns who he could or could not be for them. Instead of an outsider bringing in fences to protect animals, he recognises that the goal he shares with the local community is actually the preservation of their way of life. In order to reach that level of understanding, the relevant knowledge has to come from within the community.

This belief in the preservation of their way of life is the essence of how P10 sees himself. This is part of the unshakable commitment he has, and he is willing to change anything else to succeed in his goal. The quotes that follow illustrate how firmly this belief resonated with what he considers to be the essence of his being. P10 recognises that what he saw in the country in question was more closely aligned with what he deems essential to who he is than any business activities that he had previously undertaken.

'I guess you see it, but I think it's a matter of feeling it. You can see things, but if you don't feel it, then what you see, it may not stay with you. The day we sold the company and realised the money we were going to get, that memory is fading, but this thing with the birds is staying. It's still vivid.'

This memory about the tree being useful because the birds could sit in it stayed with him, we think, because it is aligned with who P10 believes that he was born to be. As he explained:

'When I was a boy, nature was more part of life. It was more lifestyle oriented. It's also very much my relatives. My grandparents came from a farming situation. They were basically subsistence farmers in [country] at that time. Everyone chipped in there. Everyone was part of what was going on. You couldn't opt out. You were in it, and you were living in that situation. And it was close to nature because nature provided in such ways that you, as a farmer, could sustain yourself, but you have to be in tune with nature to be able to do that. Nature can work against you if you aren't lucky and will work for you if you are lucky. So, to me, it's not a particular moment of opening the eyes to nature. I was just born into it basically.'

## A dual alignment

We can plot P10's experience with the focal community in Figure 5.1. On the horizontal axis, we can plot how far P10's activities or experiences reflect his essential self. The moment he sold his business would be closer to 'least reflective'. The experience of the conversation about the birds in the tree would be closer to 'most reflective'. This is determined by how much P10 could feel the moment and how vividly he could recall and relive it. On the vertical axis, we can plot how far activities reflect the essence of the focal community. Putting up fences is not reflective of the true essence of the community, yet protecting trees for the sole purpose of allowing the birds to enjoy them is. Framed in this way, the most meaningful philanthropic experiences occur in the intersection where they are reflective of the essence of both the community and the philanthropist is (or who the philanthropist can become).

What is interesting about this example is that it takes both P10's upbringing and his life experience, as well as the conversation he had with the community member, for him to realise who he truly is and thus that his philanthropy could be about supporting people who are good custodians of their own environment. He begins his philanthropic journey believing that he is a "nature" person and so his philanthropy should be about nature. But after an "overwhelming people experience" as he commences his journey, he realises that being able to protect a community's way of life is closer to the essence of what it means to him to be a nature person. That realisation could then find expression in what he considers to be the core of his philanthropy.

**Figure 5.1:** Alignment of essence of self and essence of community

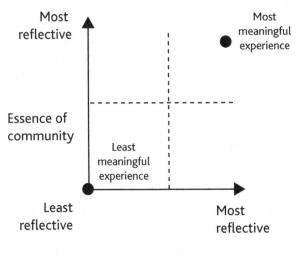

Activities at the junction between what is most reflective of the essence of the philanthropist and what is most reflective of the essence of the community deliver the greatest meaning for all. The depiction of these activities is not manufactured by P10 in isolation. Rather, it evolves from the conversations that he had with the community. Those conversations help him make sense of what he would like his philanthropy to be, and as part of that journey he is able to clarify the essence of what his life stands for.

Achieving this clarification is important, because the essence of who he is directs his philanthropic trajectory and sustains it in the face of sometimes seemingly insurmountable challenges.

> 'I've asked myself many times, why do we do it? Why do we try now as the pressure from the outside world is so relentless? It's more likely that everything collapses than you can turn it around, but, again, I guess it's also part of my upbringing. You do your best, and you have certain values, and you implement them, and you do what you believe in. Even if you're in this situation

with conservation in [continent], you may fight an uphill battle, but to me, who am I if I don't do it?'

For P10, his agentic self chooses to stick with his philanthropy because that expresses the essential self that he chooses to live as. As shown in Table 5.1, his agentic self cedes any other identities to this essential identity.

**Table 5.1:** Identity ceding to the essential self: the case of P10

| Meta-self | Experiential/ Represented selves | Agentic self | Object self |
|---|---|---|---|
| Guide the 'I' to make decisions more like a particular kind of nature person once the meta-self recognises the positive outcomes that this can create (that is, living one's essential self) even when 'I' may not succeed. | Experiential selves: nature person versus particular kind of nature person | I make the decision like a nature person or a particular kind of nature person, drawn to preserving a way of life in nature, but I do not represent myself in either of these ways.<br><br>I am willing to make more decisions like a nature person, drawn to preserving a way of life.<br>(Identity ceding) | |
| Translate an experiential agentic self into a represented agentic self so that it can be more easily accessible in the future. | Represented selves: nature person versus particular kind of nature person | I know it is the nature person who is making the decision.<br><br>I know it is a particular kind of nature person who is making the decision.<br><br>I choose to make more decisions like a nature person, drawn to preserving a way of life.<br>(Identity ceding) | I am a nature person.<br><br>I am a particular kind of nature person who is interested in preserving a way of life. |

When a person reaches this very specific understanding about what their agentic self is choosing, their meta-self may recognise that their agentic self is choosing a description of the essential self. In this case, their meta-self can be engaged to give priority to this description of the essential self in any future decisions that they might make. In P10's case, his meta-self can prioritise his essential self to guide his philanthropic decisions so that he can remain true to the essence of who he is. In this way, he can also sustain his philanthropy even in the face of near certain failure. His conviction to do the right thing does not dilute the importance of gathering evidence and measuring progress in the objective sense. To the contrary, as much evidence-based measurement as possible is employed to track the performance of his philanthropy. But the clear articulation of and conviction to his essential self means he also remains in the battle even if the evidence suggests he will fail. His sense of conviction also changes how he approaches related decision making.

> 'The me from my entrepreneurial activities would be less empathetic. It would be more results oriented. More commercialised and maybe forgetting the humanity in what we're doing or letting it play a smaller role. So I would maybe be the person then saying: "Hey, I know that what I know would benefit you." So I could go down to [continent] and just say: "I've studied, and I've experienced, and I'm going to share this with you. And, because this is good, I expect you to understand that's good for you too."
>
> And, in doing so, I forget the whole holistic situation I grew up in. And I also forget their experience of their holistic environment and how it is being bombarded and disturbed all the time with impulses from the modern world that's out there, which they don't live in but which they're exposed to.'

His decisions are shaped both by what he observes on the ground and how his sense of self is impacted by these observations. As he continues his philanthropic journey, he is reminded of the values that he grew up with and their alignment with those of the focal community. The outcome of his philanthropy may not be the successful preservation of nature in the way that he and the local community would hope for, but he can be true to who he is in how he listens to the wishes, aspirations and desires of the community and in the decisions he makes as a consequence.

## Dual alignment and the experience of philanthropy: the case of P9

In common with many of our other interviewees, P9 defines his sense of who he is based on his care for the people in his community. In his philanthropy, he intends to help the "least fortunate". Living in an emerging market, he acknowledges that he cannot help everyone, so he works hard to prioritise.

That inability to succeed in every situation does not stop him from trying whenever possible. He explained how it works in the context of supporting one of the widows that he attempted to help. P9 knew that one of his contacts could potentially interview the widow for a job, so he made the ask, but the request was turned down. This is what he shared:

> 'I know the cost of helping is very low, but it can mean a lot for someone I don't have the resources to help myself. She's a widow. She has kids. Her husband died. But she's a great secretary, so if you're looking for a secretary, you can just meet her. You can just have that interview. It's all I'm asking. Just see if she's suitable.
>
> Then, sometimes, I feel a little bit, I won't say resentful, but I feel a little bit hurt. I was the one who made the ask and then got turned down. So, yeah, I make it very much my own sometimes. They did not turn her down, but they turned me down.'

How does P9 experience this event and what implications might there be for other individuals in his community? As shown in Table 5.2, he can behave as if he is not part of the "least fortunate" community. In doing so, he would experience the rejection he faced as a rejection of another. His philanthropy would then be more sustainable, because he would not experience the hurt of

**Table 5.2**: Identity ceding from a personal to a collective identity: the case of P9

| Meta-self | Experiential/ Represented selves | Agentic self | Object self |
|---|---|---|---|
| Guide the 'I' to make decisions more like someone who is part of the community. | Experiential selves: not a part of the community versus part of the community | I make the decision as someone who is part of the community or someone who is not, but I do not represent myself in either of these ways. | |
| | | I am willing to make more decisions like someone who is part of the community. (Identity ceding) | |
| Translate an experiential agentic self into a represented agentic self so that it can be more easily accessible in the future. | Represented selves: not a part of the community versus part of the community | I know it is the person who is part of the community who is making the decision. | I am standing in rejection with the widow. |
| | | I know it is the person who is not part of the community who is making the decision. | I am an outsider looking in on others' lives. |
| | | I choose to belong even in rejection when making my next decision. (Identity ceding) | |

rejection personally. Alternatively, he can behave as if he is part of the "least fortunate" community. Then, he would experience the rejection as a personal hurt. This could make his philanthropy less sustainable, because there is more pain for him to deal with. Despite this, he purposively chooses to experience the rejection in the latter way, experiencing the hurt as a personal rejection of himself, not just a rejection of the widow.

In the ceding of his identity from one that is separate from the community to one that is at one with the community, he does not shy away from being hurt. He also does not change what he believes is the right thing to do (for example, he makes the ask in the full knowledge that he might be rejected) or minimise, in the face of the rejection, the importance to him of helping a community member (for example, he doesn't attempt to trivialise it or to say it does not matter).

He experiences the ceding of identity in his:

- *thoughts* – understanding the risks and personal hurt that may be associated with being rejected;
- *feelings* – experiencing the hurt;
- *actions* – choosing to help, standing together with the community to experience the pain of rejection;
- *being* – making choices, experiencing feelings and developing further understanding of who he is.

It is not an easy process for him: "Yeah, I am making myself vulnerable, but when you do it over and over again, it becomes, almost like … I don't wanna say it becomes second nature, because it's always difficult, but it becomes easier to do this."

As a result of what he chose to do and how he chose to experience it, he experiences a greater sense of alignment with who he is in essence.

'The more authentic we are to our values and our heart, the closer we are to God …

I believe we are children of God and that we were created in his image. If you think about that, [the idea that] you are a child of God, that means you are a piece of him. The pain he feels is the pain you feel. That's why I say it's all interconnected.

But I also believe fundamentally that we have free will, which means that, yes, you are a conduit if you want to be, but you can choose not to be and you have that free will. It's not like I'm forced to do it. I'm doing it because I want to do it. It's because I care and I'm motivated not just because of my faith but my feelings and all these things that make us human, all the things that we care about.'

He considers caring as what it means to be authentically him. He believes that caring, whether he can achieve a goal or not, is part of who he is. Living in an emerging market, he is presented every day with opportunities where he may succeed or fail in helping, but his connection to his essence sustains his efforts.

Had goal achievement been the only criterion against which to assess whether he should continue his philanthropy, the decision to continue would have been harder. However, because he also has internal criteria in play, the decision to continue is easier. As his meta-self judges that the shared goal is so aligned with his essential self and thus his purpose in life, he is able to remain true to himself and persevere.

Had the goal not been sufficiently aligned with his essential self, he would have been entirely reliant on external measures of success, with failure leading to the eventual termination of his efforts. It is important to note here that termination would have consequences both for the community and for him as a philanthropist. If his meta-self does not see the goal as sufficiently aligned with his essential self, his experience of philanthropy would be deprived of meaning and opportunities to explore his purpose in life would be missed.

It is interesting to note that the willingness to persevere is particularly marked when a moral conviction is attached to a philanthropist's chosen domain and processes. In these circumstances, they may persevere in the face of severe setbacks because that is who they believe they are born to be: a morally good person.

### Dual alignment and moral conviction: the case of P11

P11 accumulated his wealth from Wall Street. He now chairs a single-issue charity in the US. It works in a politically charged field. He shared the following:

> 'I find it incredibly bizarre that I am considered, like, the most Right-wing person on the board and yet everybody that's friends with me and involved in my political life views me as a progressive. My issue is I'm fighting to keep the board in the centre, because

the only way we're going to get effective legislation passed in this country is if more people who consider themselves Republicans care about this issue … we need their votes.

If we position ourselves and yell into the echo chamber and raise more money from the same people who intensely agree with this already, we're not going to win, and I'm just in it to win. And that is something that came from my Wall Street experience. It's like there's no second place. You just have to win.

So they're the kind of debates and that's the biggest thing I get concerned about when I'm on the board. It is necessary to be bipartisan. We're a single-issue organisation, so let's not throw ourselves in with every other progressive cause. Because we have data on our side and we're morally right. And that's only diminished by further politicising an issue that the other side wants politicised, and I don't think we should play their game.

By the way, I don't expect change to come anytime soon. I mean, not in the next five years. But how are we more thoughtful and creative to solve that problem? And as I got more involved, some people get frustrated and get burned out because it's a tough issue. You get to know a lot of these victims and survivors. You talk to politicians on both sides, and you'll find that, I'd say, at least half the Republicans in Congress and in the Senate in our country tell you privately that they are empathetic to your views but that, oh, I just couldn't vote that way or I'd get primaried by an outrageous candidate, and I found that really depressing.

I've stuck with it because, you know, it's one of those things. I have a lot of accumulated experience, like, if I don't do it, who will … both giving and time. And I'm sure there'll be others in the future, but right now I have to be that person.'

In order to help his organisation succeed in its mission, P11 has to cede what he deems to be his progressive identity, a collective political identity. He has to make decisions in a way that would be viewed as centrist by politicians, accepting that he might be deemed "Right wing" from the perspective of his board.

He puts the success of the organisation and doing what is, for him, morally right for the organisation before how he is viewed by key politicians or his board. He defines the essence of who he is by the difference he can make for others he cares about (that is, the victims and survivors) and he chooses to "be that person" even when he does not expect any change to come in the short term. Caring for those people in a bipartisan way is how he sees the essence of who he is (that is, his moral identity), and every other identity (for example, being a progressive) can be ceded in order to achieve the goals for society he shares with them.

### Integrating the unknown: the case of P12

Another shared characteristic in how our interviewees define their essence is the degree to which they are comfortable with the unknown component of who they are. Depending on their faith traditions, our interviewees describe how they experience that unknown differently. P12 summarised who he is as follows:

> 'What is true for me, again not uniquely, but somewhat, is the diversity of things that I'm involved with, from Wall Street to peace in the Middle East. There's not a lot of people who get to play on that broad playing field. I'm not unique, but I'm a member of a small group, and I'd say that one of the joys of my life is, even today, I could tell you a dozen different things I'm involved with, and I thrive on that kind of complexity, whereas others might thrive on simplicity. It's just who I am. So, I have the pleasure of being able to play to that.
>
> The complexity is oxygen for me.
>
> For most people, the creation of wealth means piling money into some bank account. For me, it's to create the resources to pursue these passions, many of which are philanthropic, but not all of them, and to have the flexibility to do that.'

Complexity for P12 is like nature for P10 and caring for P9 and P11. It is their "oxygen", as P12 put it. It is what feels natural or essential to them. For P12, his pursuit of complexity leads him to his exploration of the unknown. For him, the unknown plays a role in his choice of both process and domain.

> 'I've had my share of successes and failures. One of the things that I'm most amazed by is that a couple of the things that have failed met every one of the same tests that the things that succeeded met. And I was as excited about them as I was about the things that succeeded. It wasn't like the things that failed were stupid ideas. They felt like just as brilliant ideas as the things that succeeded.
>
> And so the world is not perfect. I couldn't figure out why they failed, because other things I had done that seemed the same were successful. And one of the things that the Serenity Prayer says is God give me the strength to change the things I can change, the equanimity to live with the things I can't change and the intelligence to know the difference.
>
> There have been a couple times where I've had to abandon projects that I was just as deeply committed to as the projects I was able to stay with. But they weren't getting traction. And, you know, when I say it that way, it's not like I would throw things away every day or something. It's not like I was flitting around, as some people accused me of, but at some point you have to give up the ghost and say: "I thought this was great, but there's a marketplace of ideas, and the market speaks, and some things we did just couldn't get traction [on]."
>
> It felt to me like sometimes we're driving the bus and sometimes we're riding a wave, and you can mix those two analogies, but the driving the bus says I don't ever want to be a victim. I want to own the fact that my life is a series of decisions which I've been lucky enough to have been able to make. I don't blame anybody else. I take full responsibility for where I am ... for better or for worse. But there are times where events, like

what's going on in Ukraine today, go and change the world. They aren't predictable. And you just have to react and do the best that you can.'

Accepting the unknown also plays out in how P12 selects his domain.

'I have a very large photographic collection, which I've been building over the last decade. It's become a huge archive of photography. But it's not clear, even though we've invested millions of dollars to build a collection on the scale of a museum, let's say, it's not clear how this will evolve, other than we think we're moving down a path.

And I had kind of a partner work with me for two years, but on a volunteer basis, who knew much more about photography than I did, but I'm more of an entrepreneur in a sense than he is, and although he had dramatically more photographic knowledge and could have done what we're now doing, it never occurred to him to do that.

We buy entire estates of photographers whose work is what we call "important but underappreciated". The reason we do that is because we think, through doing films and books and museum shows, gallery shows, sales, etc., we can lift up an entire artist's body of work, and we imagine, someday, the things we've acquired will be worth dramatically more than what we paid for them.

But we have the luxury of time, so that we're not buying something to sell it tomorrow. We're really investing. In some sense, even though I've acquired these works, I feel like the estates who sold them to us have entrusted us with their father's, or somebody's, work, knowing that we're going to work these portfolios to bring a better recognition to these artists.

And it probably isn't exactly what you were asking, but when this colleague ... joined us ... he very correctly, because he had knowledge I didn't have, questioned what we were doing. So the two of us were together one day and he said: "Well, can you describe what we're now doing?" And I said: "Yeah, what we're now doing is targeting *important but underappreciated artists.*" Now, that seems like that's just a couple of words, but it took years to evolve to that, with that level of clarity. I can talk to somebody, and when I say we're focused on important but underappreciated photographers, it conveys something in a very simple way that used to take many sentences and paragraphs and so forth. ... That eventual revelation has completely changed how we understand what we're doing.'

It took P12 years before he could clarify the meaning of his chosen domain. During those years, because of the long-term nature of the investment, he did not necessarily have the external successes needed to provide evidence to support his decision to keep growing the collection. He functioned based on his conviction about who he is and how his processes work. For him, there will always be unknowns that can potentially fuel him with complexity, and he is content to let that complexity emerge. During the early years of building the collection, he had to cede the part of him who was curious to know what this collection is about to the part of him whose essence is comfortable with the unknown.

This example also provides us further insight into how identity ceding works. The process begins with understanding how people experience and define who they are in their object and agentic selves. In P12's example, his object self can be defined in the following ways:

- I am someone who thrives on complexity; or
- I am someone whose essential self thrives on complexity.

The second definition is more complex than the first, and it signifies a different level of understanding our sense of who we are. For P12, the second object self has a much better chance of being selected to be the agentic self that influences decisions when those decisions are deemed important to the individual.

The agentic self is both the knower and the chooser, and the content and nature of the agentic self can grow more complex as more of the essence of who we are is recognised through the decisions we make. Thus, in P12's case, we might define the content of the agentic self in a number of different ways.

- I know I am the person who thrives on complexity.
- I know my essential self is the person who thrives on complexity.
- I choose my essential self as the person who thrives on complexity over my other identities.
- I choose my essential self to be the person who thrives on complexity which includes the unknown.

As our thoughts, feelings, actions and ways of being settle into recognisable patterns, our represented agentic self can morph. As our agentic self develops and becomes more complex, so too can our meta-self.

For P12, the processes engaged in by his meta-self may include:

- recognising each time his agentic self chooses his essential self to make a decision;
- recognising the object selves his agentic self rejects in order to make a decision consistent with his essential self;
- monitoring any modifications in the nature of the agentic and object self every time he makes a selection or rejection;
- identifying modifications that appear consistent with the essential self and facilitating that essential self's subsequent reinforcement and prioritisation in decision making;
- accepting the unknown in the decision making engaged in by the agentic self and recognising its role in shaping the true self.

Given the complexity of the situations that P12 shared, he was asked how he gained the confidence and had the assurance that he should embrace the unknown. He shared the following:

> 'I literally don't think there's an answer, other than that one has to be open to hearing an inner voice and to cultivating it. And I've done that through meditation practice for long periods of my adult life. In particular, now, for the last decade, I have a daily meditation practice and have been in analysis, which is another

form of exploration, ranging from three to five days a week over the last 12 years.

And I think you have to have perhaps a model of how your psyche or your brain works. You could either use Freud's model of the id, the super id and the ego or just call it the unconscious and the conscious. ... One part is in the moment, in the here and now, reacting to stimuli, and another part is working in the background, processing. It supplies more strategic information. That may not be the right word, but the point is that many times when I'm meditating, something will come into my head about something that I wanted to do, something that I'm inspired to do, something I forgot to do.

It comes from a place that's different from where I get what I need to just function at work during the day and think things out.

So, I'm not claiming any particular unique thing other than that, when people tap into some inner voice that speaks to their own calling or their own truth, it allows for some kind of *organising principle of one's life* that's different from when you're just running from one opportunity to the next.'

When this process is taken into account, we can further redefine P12's sense of self. His object self could be:

someone who navigates complexity by anchoring on an inner voice while taking into consideration available external stimuli.

His agentic self can then choose to behave as this particular object self over any object self that navigates complexity by anchoring on an inner voice alone or by relying on external stimuli alone. When he chooses this object self, his agentic self may also become aware that his essential self thrives when he navigates complexity in this, but not other, ways.

The process engaged by his meta-self may then include:

• recognising the precise circumstance under which the agentic self chooses one object self over another;

- monitoring how the agentic self chooses the object self and whether this process needs to be modified;
- if modification is required, identifying whether the modification is consistent with the essential self;
- if the modification is consistent with the essential self, facilitating its subsequent reinforcement and prioritisation in decision making;
- accepting the unknown in the decision making engaged in by the agentic self and managing its role in shaping the essential self.

Being attuned to their essential self shapes people's choices of what domains and processes are theirs. It also impacts how much people can focus and sustain their decisions once they have chosen their domains and processes. In some situations, they have feedback from the community to help guide their way (for example, P8). In others, the feedback is partial (for example, P9, P10 and P11), while in yet others there may be a long wait to receive any feedback at all (for example, P12). The unknown can thus be more or less significant in sustaining decisions.

It took 14 years before P8 was convinced his business would succeed, and he was 10 years into his philanthropy before he was convinced that his processes (volunteerism) would work well in his selected domain (youth education). He was thus managing unknowns for an extended period of time. Similarly, P10 shopped around, considering many charities, with only the sense that he was a "nature" person, not knowing at that point how his essence would play out. For P12, his caring and cognisance of the unknown factored into his actions for over a decade.

Table 5.3 summarises our preceding discussion and provides a snapshot of the essence of self that developed during the philanthropic experience of our interviewees. It looks too at the identities that were ceded to create community benefit. As should by now be clear, identity ceding and the recognition of one's essential self are both gradual processes that happen over an extended period of time. It is also important to acknowledge that what can be captured in each snapshot paints only a very partial picture of how people experience their philanthropy. But the examples do offer a window on the role of different forms of self and their relationship with enhanced community benefit.

**Table 5.3:** Identity ceding, the essential self and community benefit

|  | Identity ceded | Essence of self developed or explored | Community benefit |
|---|---|---|---|
| P6 | A childhood trauma survivor | A regenerative adult capable of mentoring others during crises that trigger trauma | Mentees receiving the financial, psychological, social and spiritual support they need |
| P8 | King of my enterprise | A sensitive listener and a member of the community | An extended family with educational opportunities through activism |
| P9 | An individual separate from the community they help | A communal identity as part of a focal community | A "least fortunate" community continuing to receive support through numerous challenges |
| P10 | A nature person | A nature person who cares about preserving a custodian's way of life with nature | A community supported in their way of being/living with nature |
| P11 | A political progressive | A political centrist caring for victims and survivors | Political consensus and eventual change |
| P12 | Someone who thrives on the complexity of the known | Someone who thrives on navigating the complexity created by the unknown | Important but underappreciated artists eventually receiving the appreciation their importance warrants |

What marks the way interviewees navigate alignment between the essential self and community need in the face of the unknown is the directionality of how they change their sense of their essential self. Whenever they encounter situations in which they needed to cede their identities to move themselves and the community closer to their shared goal, that is what they do.

## Conclusion

In this chapter, we defined the concept of the essential self and explored how this self can be part of one's identity ceding process. We provided examples of how our interviewees manage the changing of their identity and the process of discovery of their essential self in the context of the unknown. We also illustrated how their essential self provides them with the tenacity they needed to create social realities that might otherwise have been impossible to create (for example, P8's community centre, P12's art collection and P10's chance to preserve a way of life for future generations).

Benefits to the community aside, the creation of these new social realities provides (simultaneously) new ways in which they can experience their essential self. Our philanthropists are exploring what could be most meaningful for them in what they do, taking account of the unknown. In simple terms, who they truly are can embrace additional layers of meaning as well as a level of meaningfulness that would not otherwise have been possible. This potential for discovery could be why they never experience either process as self-sacrificial.

As layers of meaning develop, how meaningful each philanthropic experience can be for both the individual and the community will grow. This growth is not created only by what impact or how much impact is made, but by making sense of the following questions in the context of one's philanthropy:

- What is the essence of my focal community?
- What is the essence of my life?
- How can alignment between my life essence and the community help us both recognise something about us that neither of us knew before?
- How do these issues contribute to the sense of meaning and meaningfulness delivered by philanthropy?

We develop our understanding of meaning and meaningfulness in Chapter 6.

# 6

# Meaning and meaningfulness

People are actively motivated to make sense of the information presented by the context around them (Baumeister and Vohs, 2002). Yet we do not understand much about how *meaning* is derived in philanthropy. In previous chapters, we outlined the choices that people make in their philanthropy, the way they define their sense of self in the context of these activities and how some, in the ceding of their existing identities, can experience an increased understanding of who they are and their essential self.

As they progress in their journey of discovering the alignment between their essential self and the essence of the community, they are also learning to accept the unknown, both in their environment and in their essential self. They gradually gain confidence in what they can achieve, and they learn to trust the iterative process that they go through in order to create a greater collective good.

All of this sets up the context for us to explore how meaning is created through our interviewees' philanthropic journeys and how they experience a sense of *meaningfulness* during this process. Without this background, we could not take our discussion to the kind of meaning that seems to matter most in growing and sustaining philanthropy.

As we explore this topic, we do not assume that people carry out philanthropic activities in an explicit search for meaning. To the contrary, when people begin their philanthropic activities, they are usually focused on developing a vision for how the world could be made better for the various stakeholders they care about. It is not a search for personal meaning per se.

We learned through our interviews that what originally motivates people to do something is often not what ultimately supplies meaning for them. For some, the meaning arises from becoming aware of challenges they have not previously encountered. They thus gain additional insights into what they are capable of achieving. Others become aware of how they need to cede their sense of who they are in order to achieve the goals they share with a community. Thus, they discover new meaning in terms of both who they are themselves and the nature of the community they care about. Still others find meaning in continuing the 'right' course of action even in the face of considerable difficulty. Our interviews suggest that this latter source of meaning could be among the most meaningful the individuals encountered in their life to date.

What interviewees' experiences have in common is that the meaning that can derive from philanthropy is often not something that can be discovered until after the journey begins. This suggests an opportunity for greater reflection on how meaning might be experienced, which in turn can be used to generate a road map that can sensitise those new to the field to potential benefits that might hitherto have been obscured. The richer the meaning derived from philanthropy, the more likely it is that philanthropy can be appropriately shaped and sustained.

It turns out that meaning and meaningfulness are concepts that have been researched recently in the fields of psychology (King and Hicks, 2021), management (Rosso et al, 2010; Bailey et al, 2019; Lysova et al, 2019) and leadership (Winton et al, 2022). Here, we define these terms, explore the our interviewees' experiences in relation to the concepts and conclude by illustrating how conscious reflection on these topics can indeed be helpful in sustaining an individual's philanthropy.

## Meaning

Pratt and Ashforth (2003: 310) define meaning as the 'output of having made sense of something or what it signifies'. In relation to our topic, this sense could be derived from how people interpret what their philanthropy means for themselves and others.

'Meaning' and 'purpose' are often used as synonyms (Martela and Steger, 2016).

One school of thought in the academy suggests that perceptions of meaning are ultimately determined by the individual (Baumeister, 1991). This psychological perspective grants agency to individuals surrounded by many potential sources of meaning to determine what is meaningful for themselves.

A different school of thought suggests that meaning is constructed socially, deriving from compliance with norms, shared perceptions of experience or both (Pratt and Ashforth, 2003). Scholars in this tradition thus propose that one's philanthropic experiences are deemed meaningful when the social and cultural systems around people support that conclusion.

Our interviewees also seem to experience meaning in another, somewhat different, way. Consistent with the two schools of thought described here, they consider meaning as the output of making sense of something, whether influenced by the social context or not. In either case, meaning results from some form of appraisal. But our interviewees also seem to find meaning in the process of discovering what may or may not offer meaning. Thus, P8 can derive meaning by becoming part of the family at the core of his community, but he can also derive meaning from the process of discovering that this is both possible and desirable. He can also derive meaning from the journey toward family.

This experience of meaning does not take the social norms or shared perceptions associated with 'family' as a static set of rules and principles that one needs to accept. Rather, it treats the community that P8 cedes his identity to as a changeable collective in which new social norms and shared perceptions can emerge. This emergence itself offers P8 a rich sense of meaning.

In the remainder of this chapter, we explore a variety of perspectives on meaning creation and attempt to categorise them.

## Meaning creation: the case of P13

After a successful career as the CEO of one of the world's leading consumer goods companies, P13 created his own non-profit organisation to grow a community of like-minded business leaders committed to the betterment of society. P13 explained the source of what draws him to do what he does:

> 'The source [of my giving] comes from realising how lucky I was. My parents had food at home, so I wasn't stunted. Now, there are 160 million children stunted because they don't get enough nutrition in the first 1,000 days. I had a piece of bar soap at home, so I didn't die of infectious diseases like pneumonia or diarrhoea, like four million children do before they're eight, or five.
>
> My parents couldn't afford it, as my father worked in a factory, but I had free education from the government. So, I realised a long time ago I wouldn't be talking to you if I had not won the lottery ticket of life by being born in a wealthy country.'

P13's giving does not stem only from the fact that human suffering exists at a large scale. Neither is it entirely the consequence of his upbringing. Instead, it derives from the way that he assigns meaning to his own life in the context of the lives of others.

In respect of his upbringing, he noted:

> 'Obviously, it's always where you grow up and the messages you get from your parents. You know, my parents were deprived of their education because of the Second World War, and for them it was absolutely important that there was peace in Europe and that we got a better education than they had and that the communities in which they worked function. So, you get some values that drive you, that guide you on your purpose if you want them to.'

His parents created the social environment that he grew up in and the value system to which he was exposed. As he grew up, he could choose to accept these as his own or he could choose to reject them, instead charting his own course. Consistent with the first school of thought mentioned earlier, in the absence of his agency, neither option can contribute to the meaning he ascribes to his life.

## *Meaning experienced from ceding one's singular self to a collective*

Where P13's approach differs from the first school of thought, we think, is in how he assigns meaning to his own life in the context of his specific social environment. He does not choose to merely be influenced by the environment; he chooses to be part of it.

This "being together", as P13 put it, is experienced in and of itself as meaning, regardless of whether he can ultimately make sense of why he and others in the social environment are together and what they might create together.

> 'I think it's at the end. You know the concept of "ubuntu" in Africa, which says "I am because we are" – our own sense of purpose has to come from being part of a broader system on which we depend … I think everybody has crucibles in their lives that connect them to that deeper purpose.'

P13 sees his philanthropy as his way of connecting to his deeper purpose, or what we term the essential self. This does not mean that he must arrive at that deeper purpose before he can experience meaning. Every experience of connecting to something deeper can also be experienced as meaning.

Though process is important, we do not mean to imply that there are no guiding principles that shape how he can experience meaning. He makes sense of his life based broadly on the contrast between what he received and what others did not receive, and how he relates to those others. He characterises the relationship as one of dependence, but interestingly not one that regards the community as dependent on him. Quite the opposite. He depends on community to experience meaning.

Facilitating others to achieve their potential provides him a rich sense of meaning. Being someone who can help in this way is core to the meaning he assigns to his life. It allows him to embrace the pursuit of community benefit and experience any gains as his own. When facilitating others as part of 'we' is the purpose he assigns to his life, any difference between him and others in the same 'we' then becomes the source of his drive to help.

Interestingly, because of the depth of the personal relationships he has with many in the community, the magnitude of the need does not dull the intensity of his connection to the community. It should also be noted that the level of need doesn't overwhelm him. Instead, it compels him to become more deliberate and focused on opportunities with the capacity to impact at scale.

> 'I was asked by Ban Ki-moon, the [then UN] Secretary General, to help develop the Sustainable Development Goals, and I was representing the business community. I was drinking from a fire hose. That was an enormous learning to get to my purpose, to listen to all these parts of society ... people with disabilities, minorities, indigenous people, youths and farmers, and the list goes on. What were their dreams and ideas?'

Consistent with the second school of thought on meaning, the social and cultural values that P13 is exposed to through his role at the United Nations (UN) shape what he considers to be his "purpose".

## *Meaning experienced from the process of sense making and self-transformation*

For P13, the process of 'listening' and 'getting to know' his purpose infuses as much meaning into his experience as finally being able to articulate his purpose. Who he is, who he will be and what he considers essential for him all morph as meaning is created. He willingly allows the communities he encounters to shape his sense of who he is, experiencing the transformation itself as deeply meaningful.

P13 offered an example:

> 'I climbed Mount Kilimanjaro with blind people, because I had a blind friend and we decided to take people from all parts of the world. We took the highest number of blind people up Kilimanjaro, including the first blind African [to climb the mountain], but it changed my life again in thinking about it's not

people with disabilities, but rather different abilities and capabilities.'

As who he is changes, so too does his perception of his social environment. His social environment does not present as a static set of norms or shared perceptions. Rather, the nature of that environment can change. The nature of what he chooses to see in that environment can also change. His perception shifts away from seeing "people with disabilities" to seeing people with "different abilities and capabilities". The change is highly significant, since perceiving the community as disabled defines it in such a way that is very difficult for him to feel part of (that is, because he is "abled"). But in defining it as a community of people with different abilities and capabilities, P13 can readily become part of the community and derive meaning from the consequent transformation process.

When meaning is created in this way, P13 considers connection with the community an integral part of how he lives his life. Maintaining that connection is not something he does only through his philanthropy; he does this through other facets of his life too.

'I've personally always tried to just stay very close to the realities of the world and not get sucked into the bubble of the CEO wealth. You know, we didn't have private planes. I move in public transportation. All my brothers and sisters have normal jobs, you know. We live in a normal house. We don't seclude ourselves from the world. We think it's important to be part of anybody.'

In this example, consistent with the first school of thought, P13 exercises his agency. He chooses between the values he wants his life to reflect: those drawn from the bubble of CEO wealth or those from what he sees as the realities of the world.

*Meaning experienced from the process of creating a new social reality*

Different from the second school of thought, P13's agency is not exercised for the purpose of conforming to a social norm. Rather, he selects norms that allow him to get closer to his purpose. Thus, for example, he lives his family life in a way that allows him to experience his wider community ties in a personal way.

Consistent with the second school of thought, his selected social norms and his conformity to them could be experienced as meaning. But meaning can also be experienced through the selection process itself.

Even with P13's modest lifestyle and his intention that he and his family remain rooted in reality, the differences between his lived experience and the lived experience of his focal community are still so great that it is not possible for him to fully adopt the perspective of his community or empathise to the extent that he can feel precisely what others feel. However, that tension between what it is possible to experience and what is desirable to experience does not stop him from taking action. Nor does the tension hurt his ability to experience meaning. The realisation that a gap exists, and every effort to reduce it, can potentially be meaningful.

P13 uses compassion to bridge the gap between what he can experience and what he cannot. He said: "Empathy and compassion are two different words. I can never really fully feel what others are feeling, but I can help make changes in the environment in which they operate to give them better opportunities. I can also show dignity and respect. I can fight for equity."

Compassion, in the psychology literature (Goetz et al, 2010; Oveis et al, 2010), is defined as one's urge to care for someone or something when they are in distress. The feeling of compassion can urge people into action without them having to fully understand what the distress is or how it is experienced by others. They simply take the action necessary to help alleviate the distress and close the gap. But in P13's case, his actions are so influential that they can help form a new social reality: a world that achieves Sustainable Development Goals versus a world that does not.

If P13's only reason for choosing to work with the UN was to conform to social norms, then the meaning derived from the experience would be different from the meaning offered if takes the action as a consequence of the compassion he feels for those who might benefit.

The second school of thought in meaning could have predicted the former source of meaning (that is, conformity to a norm) but not the latter (that is, the meaning accruing from his deliberative sense of compassion).

## Meaning experienced from moments that "stick"

Another element of the experience of meaning that we want to highlight using the experience of P13 is what he termed "*moments that stick with you*". He described them this way:

'And then, during life, you have *some moments that stick with you*. For example, when I worked in [city], shipbuilding, steel and coal had gone belly up, bankrupt. So I saw, for the first time, second-generation unemployment, and, you know, the only thing a 16-year-old girl could get was pregnant. That was, then, her dignity or respect.

But, making matters worse, we were the biggest employers, so I really felt we had to get into these communities to make it work. That gets to my deeper purpose of making the [UN] Sustainable Development Goals come alive: to apply yourself to the service of others, knowing that by doing so, you're better off yourself as well.'

He does not select which moments would "stick" with him. They just do. In this sense, one could argue that he did not have agency to 'choose' those moments; he just recognises them as creating meaning for him.

Those moments then direct not only the immediate actions he takes when they first occur; they also direct how he acts sometimes years later and when acting in very different capacities. These moments are important because when he becomes aware of their influence, he experiences a 'coming alive' or energising of his own purpose in life.

We think this moment P13 experiences is similar to what P8 experiences with the birds and what P12 experiences with his "*important but underappreciated artists*". These moments all make an impression. Their memories all seem to stick, remain vivid and propel the individuals into taking their lives in a particular direction. It is important to remember, though, that the meaning assigned to these moments can change and be developed over time.

Earlier in his life, P13 experienced a sticky moment when he realised the impact of second-generation unemployment and came face to face with the depth of despair it could create. That moment was deeply meaningful to him, because he was then able to recognise the urgency for his organisation (and for him personally) to help tackle despair in the community. He found meaning in being able to return hope.

Later in his life, he is able to see the parallels between this earlier circumstance and being asked to assist in the development of the UN Sustainable Development Goals. Reflection on his earlier "moment" energises his desire to deliver hope at a hugely more significant scale. When his moment is relevant to guiding or energising the accomplishment of new tasks, he is able to layer new meaning onto his original experience all those years earlier.

In this example, meaning is enriched for P13 when he recognises the parallel between two experiences and draws strength from one to tackle or energise the other. Meaning could be enriched P13 by how he chooses what to see in a given moment.

'I was in Mumbai when the attack happened on the Taj Mahal and people around us were losing their lives. We were fortunate to be spared. I don't know why, but I saw the cost of terror but also the goodness in people.

I go around a lot in the emerging markets. That's where [my company] had 60 per cent of its business, and that's where most of the growth is, but I always would go into people's homes and, often, the poorest of the poorest. And you see how they live, how generous they are, what aspirations they have.'

P13 doesn't understand why he sees "the cost of terror" but at the same time recognises "the goodness in people". But this way of seeing can be intuitive if we trace the process of how he chooses to make sense of his life through the communities he encounters. There is a clear directionality in how he sees others. It appears to move beyond what they do not have to what they do have. We do not know if he would have seen in the same way if he had not chosen to "stay very close to the realities of the world" and to experience compassion beyond the limitations of empathy. All that we can say is that when he chooses to live his life in this particular way, he acts in the following way: "Sometimes, with fairly simple things, you can actually understand and unlock major things in their lives as well ... sometimes by listening, sometimes by touching, sometimes by giving, you create this multiplier effect."

The distinction between the meaning derived from experience and the process of experiencing that meaning is, we think, important. A focus on the latter furnishes individuals with a way to maximise the meaning they can experience from their philanthropy before they reach the point of being able to articulate what they can actually achieve. It also provides an alternative way for people to steer their philanthropic effort and create the kind of social reality that is impossible to see at the start of their philanthropic journey.

## Meaning associated with self

In the previous section, we defined as both the sense made of something and the process of making sense of it. We illustrated this division with the experience of P13. We now take our reflection to the next level and map these experiences of meaning onto the five components of self.

As we saw in previous chapters, how people define their sense of who they are is highly subjective (Walker and Frimer, 2007; McAdams, 2011). People subjectively assign labels to themselves and define what these labels mean, and live out these labels and definitions in their thoughts, feelings and actions, without explicitly representing themselves as such. We used object and agentic self versus experiential and represented self to characterise these different components of self.

When people engage in philanthropic activities, especially if these activities span extended periods of time, the meaning they experience from them will eventually overlap with the meaning they associate with their sense of who they are. This occurs even if they choose explicitly to not let their philanthropy define who they are. In those cases, their sense of who they are would be defined by their choice of how they do *not* define themselves. In all the interviews that we carried out, however, people did seem to welcome the opportunity to define their sense of who they are through their philanthropic activities. We rely primarily on the experience of P13 again to map out how meaning can be experienced through different elements of self.

## Meaning experienced from object self

At the lowest level of complexity, P13 can define his sense of who he is by the simplest relationships that he experiences and the most straightforward representations. He can make sense of who he is as an object self: he is a son born to his parents; he is a citizen born into a wealthy country; he is an employee of different employers in different social circumstances; he is a representative of the business community for the development of the UN Sustainable Development Goals. All these definitions are reflected by the collective identity labels that he wears, be it son, citizen, employee or representative.

In the simplest experience of meaning, he adopts these labels together with the norms, shared perceptions, expectations and understandings associated with them. They then guide his behaviour. Hence, the meaning of his philanthropy is about how he conforms to what he chooses to adopt in his object selves.

## Meaning experienced from agentic self

P13 can also make sense of who he is as an agentic self who is a knower and a chooser. In his experiential agentic self, he can choose to behave like a son or a representative without necessarily labelling himself as such or clarifying the associated definitions. In his represented agentic self, he knows what labels he uses to describe himself and how he defines 'I'. He then chooses how he behaves based on which representation will dominate in shaping the behaviour. He knows, for example, that as a son, he can draw on the values from his parents, and that when he is behaving in ways consistent with these values, he is living his sonship. Similarly, he knows that as an employee of a particular employer, he can choose to care for his subordinates in ways that conform to the social norms and shared perceptions of that employer.

In the simplest experience of meaning associated with agentic self, there is only one label that he can adopt in each situation, and he simply follows the representation prescribed by that one label. When he is at home, he behaves like a son; when he is at work, he behaves like an employee; and when he is at the UN, he behaves like a representative of the business community. He acts in accordance with the labels or representations that his agentic self adopts, and that provides the meaning that he experiences.

But his sense of self becomes more complex when it involves the agentic self taking the initiative to define what these collective identity labels mean or choose between which labels or definitions to behave in accordance with. For example, as he chooses to listen to the people he interacts with, he can choose to listen to them as a son of his parents, as an employee of his various employers or as a representative working with the UN. When exposed to armed conflict, whether he was seeing his surroundings as a son, an employee or a representative, he could choose to see either terror or the goodness of people faced with terror. He could choose to associate different ways of seeing with each one of these labels and then define these labels differently based on his lived experience. What he sees then changes how he chooses to behave and the social environment he will consequentially interact with. The trajectory of not only his philanthropy, but his career and personal life can consequentially change.

In these more complex situations, meaning can emerge from what he eventually chooses to label himself, how he defines this label, and how he behaves and what he creates when he acts in this manifestation of self. Meaning can also emerge from the process of how he is choosing. Both can contribute to the meaning he experiences in his philanthropy.

When people say things like 'I do not think about myself in my philanthropy; I only think about other people', they are making a statement about who their experiential agentic self is. Their agentic self makes a decision to see themselves and their relationship with others in a certain way, and then they behave accordingly.

They do not label themselves as selfless and they do not represent themselves as being selfless, but their experiential agentic self behaves in a selfless way. In such circumstances, they are not, strictly speaking, selfless. Their agentic self is still there. It simply chooses not to give itself a label. This experiential agentic self can still experience meaning through its choices.

Our research suggests that these selfless individuals will be better served by reflecting on who their agentic self is than not paying this any attention. This is because they will have an opportunity to purposefully develop it into one that might be even more effective in achieving the collective goal. This loss may become even more costly in situations where interventions from the meta-self might be necessary in order to resolve conflicts blocking the achievement of collective goals. We explore this next.

## Meaning experienced from meta-self

People's sense of self present in their philanthropy become even more complex when it involves the meta-self choosing between different definitions for its agentic self, choosing different agentic selves to prioritise, and recognising what it considers to be the essence of 'I' and 'we' and prioritising accordingly. It is possible that in these situations, different agentic selves will guide their behaviour in conflicting or opposing directions, and their meta-self has to override the choice made by one agentic self with a choice made by another. We saw many instances of this when our interviewees chose to cede, for example, their king, childhood trauma survivor and limited human being selves to their sensitive listener, regenerative adult and human channel of unlimited love selves.

Given that the meta-self is about managing and resolving conflicts between selves, the meaning people experience with their meta-self is rarely just about which agentic self is most effective in particular situations. Rather, the meta-self has to manage all the contextual details (and associated meanings) that can inform the decision about when one agentic self should be selected over another. This process is complex, because the meaning people experience from one part of their life can interact with the meaning they experience from other parts. The meaning they experience from their philanthropy can also shape the meaning they experience from the personal and professional aspects of their lives. It is, of course, possible for people to develop a 'philanthropist' identity that is isolated from all their other identities, but we rarely saw evidence of this in our interviews. Rather, the interviewees experience their philanthropy as object and agentic selves that are much more broadly constructed than the narrow philanthropic self.

We saw this most clearly in the experiences of P6 and P9, where their philanthropic experience becomes one in which they can push the boundaries and become the kind of regenerative adult and human channel of unlimited love that no other aspect of their lives could have let them become. The development of the meta-self through philanthropic experience can cross-fertilise meaning to benefit other aspects of life.

## How can we create the most meaning-filled philanthropic experiences?

The meaning that people experience in their philanthropy is driven in part by the elements of self that are at the table. The exact same external impact can create very different meaning experiences for different kinds of people. The impact is also experienced differently based on how these different kinds of people recognise and manage the unknown.

What all this suggests is that we can almost never a *priori* describe the actual meaning that a person can experience in their philanthropy. This has profound implications for fundraisers, who traditionally develop a case for support based around the need that may be met. This is usually based on shared visions and a set of programme outcome descriptions which track impact on the community. Rarely, if ever, are the impacts on the philanthropist considered, specifically the selves that experience the delivery of this impact.

The futility of the approach is also laid bare by our enhanced understanding of the sources and roles of meaning. Fundraisers should be considering not only the selves they are addressing, but also how those selves experience meaning. While meaning can certainly be generated through the achievement of goals, it can equally well be created through the experience of the journey towards those goals. If fundraisers are sensitive to the process through which meaning emerges, they can facilitate access to it. They can ensure that no source of potential meaning is missed and, specifically, no opportunity to experience meaning through transformation is neglected.

To summarise, our research suggests that we can maximise meaning during the philanthropic journey by supporting the process as well as the outcome of the meaning experience. We can do so by exploring with philanthropists:

- who and what they care about in the context of their philanthropy;
- what relationships they have (or need) with those they care about;
- how they define their sense of self, particularly in their social environment;
- how they create meaning in the context of their different selves in this social environment;
- how they interact with and shape their social environment; and
- how these changes consequentially change a collective definition of who they are and the precise nature of their social environment.

To go deeper, we support the individual's philanthropic journey by:

- understanding how they make identity choices, the labels they append to these identities and the characteristics of these identities;
- recognising that the sticky moments – the ones that remain with people for extensive periods of time – vividly and powerfully steer the direction of their actions;
- supporting their life journey towards a clearer and clearer articulation of their essence and that of their community, while keeping in mind that the unknown will always play a part.

When applying these principles, we need to keep in mind that for some people meaning can be sourced only from their neurological, psychological and social environments, while for others their journeys are deeply spiritual.

## Meaningfulness

Meaningfulness refers to the amount of significance something holds for an individual (Pratt and Ashforth, 2003). It is a sense that the meaning one experiences in a moment is not trivial and that it matters (Martela and Steger, 2016). If meaning denotes the 'what' and the 'how' of our philanthropic experience, meaningfulness denotes how significant our 'what' and 'how' is.

Similar to the experience of meaning, what is meaningful for each individual is also deeply subjective. The same meaning may be perceived as extremely meaningful by one individual and not very meaningful by another. The moment of selling his business is trivial for P10, but the moment of the birds is significant. For other interviewees, their business experience has been much more meaningful than their philanthropic experience.

Our interviewees recognise the significance of these moments by:

- how vividly they can remember these experiences of meaning;
- how long the memory of these vivid experiences lasts;
- the impact these experiences of meaning have on shaping the trajectory of choices they can make and the social environment they encounter;
- the impact that these vivid meaning experiences have on the way they think and feel in the here and now;
- the impact that these vivid meaning experiences have on defining their sense of who they are;
- the degree to which these vivid meaning experiences confirm what they know already about their purpose in life;
- the degree to which meaning can help them explore novel understanding about the essence of their lives.

In the context of philanthropy, these meaningful moments always involve at least one interaction with another person. Very often, they involve the interaction the person has with a community.

Similar to the experience of meaning, the experience of meaningfulness is also a process. Sometimes we have control over this process, while other times we do not. Very often, the significance of meaning takes years, if not decades, to develop. Along the way, the meaning we experience can only be as meaningful as what we are able to recognise at those moments in time.

We illustrate this process with another experience P13 shared with us. It is an example of where he has control over how much meaningfulness he can experience from a moment of meaning he creates.

P13 shared:

> 'I went to visit a home in Bangladesh where there was nothing, no money in the family, but she [the lady in the house] made a beautiful face with flowers made from plastic and waste, that I still have in my house on the kitchen counter, and I keep it there.'

The meaning that P13 assigns to this piece of art is described in the following: "It's not the nicest or most beautiful object, but in a sense, *it is* the most beautiful object because it comes from the heart. It comes from real people." That is how he makes sense of this gift. That is the meaning that he assigns to it. But that statement does not capture the meaning that he experiences through the process of how he interacts with the gift, or the significance associated with it.

On being offered this gift, he has the option of receiving it or not receiving it. Social norms and shared perceptions in that circumstance would require that he receive the gift. It would have been rude not to. That being the case, the only meaning he could experience from that gift flows from adherence to the social norm. This meaning then may or may not be very meaningful for him, because he does not exercise much autonomy in accepting the gift. His agentic self does not have a choice to make, and it does not impact on his sense of who he is.

But we can imagine a different scenario where he brings the gift to his hotel room. At that point, he is not subject to the same social scrutiny, so he could choose to pack or not pack the gift in his suitcase. The meaning that he assigns to this gift has to be meaningful enough that he takes the personal initiative to pack the gift into his suitcase and bring it back home. In so doing, he can begin to experience the ownership he takes over the meaning of the gift. This process of taking ownership is also experienced as meaning, and can be deeply meaningful.

But we have yet to capture the full significance of the gift he experiences. After he brought the gift home, he kept it on his kitchen counter for what is now over a decade. He is still looking at this piece of art every day. What he chooses to stick with him will contribute to how meaningful this piece of art and this experience can be in his life. In this case, "the most beautiful object ... from real people" is the meaning he experiences as meaningful. But so is his decision to keep it for such a long time and cherish it in his day-to-day life.

## Encountering significance: the case of P14

P14's experience of significance is not controlled or initiated by her. It nevertheless shares many of the same characteristics as P13's gift experience. P14's experience began when she visited a ten-year-old boy who was rescued from a life as a child soldier.

> 'I can remember once standing next to a ten-year-old boy who, you know, he'd been seeing his parents killed. He'd been forced to kill another child from his village. He had escaped from the army. He came back and he had been placed in a rehabilitation centre.
>
> We found an auntie in another village a long way away that would take him, because he couldn't go back to his other village, because he killed another child there. So, I know this is what this boy had been through.
>
> But, as he is standing there, he's ten years old, and this ... still upsets me [starts to cry].
>
> Some of the emotions are always there. I had a ten-year-old son at home [continues to cry].
>
> I had a ten-year-old son at home, and I'm thinking *this is my child* ...
>
> This happened 20 years ago.
>
> Yeah, so, it's like this child could have been my child ... *he, he was my child.*'

Very often, when our interviewees shared moments like these, they could not articulate how the experience took on a high level of significance in their lives. Such moments of recognition are not something that they intentionally seek. Very often, until these moments occur, the person does not know that these experiences exist.

Once they encounter those moments, however, the significance is not lost on them, and it can develop over time. The continuing process was described by P14:

> 'When I reflect on it, at the time, it wasn't upsetting for me, because I knew he was going to go to his auntie. But when I got home, when I was back with my children, that's when the impact hit me.
>
> And [reflecting on her crying] obviously it still does 20 years later.
>
> And that's just the impact that, you know, one thing can have on you. Yeah, but at the time, I didn't realise the impact.
>
> But, in fact, I think it's a really good thing that although I haven't spoken about this for a long, long time ... even after all this time, it can still have this emotional impact on me.'

Although research suggests that when a sense of meaningfulness is experienced, it is typically associated with a positive feeling, this does not mean that there cannot be scenarios experienced as bittersweet or as a combination of negative and positive, as we can see from P14's description.

Although our interviewee sobs, it is not a sense of sadness per se that she experiences. It is more a sense of being deeply moved. The experience matters to her. It is not trivial. It provides her with a sense of connection to the community she supports – a community that she has connected with as her own family.

She went on to say that this connection grounds all her decision-making processes, including those that play out in the board room. Difficult decisions may need to be made, and while she can still make them rationally, based on evidence, the process is infused with love and care in the very real knowledge that they will have consequences for boys just like her son.

The level of significance she experiences in relation to the child soldier is enhanced by her experience with her own children. The significance of both can then be transferred to her board room decisions. However, she does not fully recognise this significance until she encounters intensity of emotion during the interview. It is possible that her experience of significance will continue to grow as moments like these continue to occur.

### Deepening meaning: the case of P15

P15 is a 28-year-old, fifth-generation wealth inheritor. She has spent six years working with women and girls who were trafficked into the sex trade in the developing world. Reflecting on the meaning of her life, she shared the following:

'I could compare and contrast living in San Francisco as a student with endless pocket money versus living in Mexico as a social worker. There has to be a reason why I made the choice I did. I just knew that I wouldn't be able to live with myself if I had left them.

Yeah, I'm not a survivor of sex trafficking, but I'm a woman, you know. I hope to be a mom. I was someone's child. I'm someone's daughter. I'm Asian, and I know that I'm feminised, you know, universally, by being an Asian woman. And I've had terrifying experiences of my own despite being as privileged and as sheltered as I am. It happens all the time.

But my purpose is so far beyond just me. It actually brings me comfort that it has nothing to do with me, you know, that it's not about me as an individual but me in a sort of abstract sense of the different hyphenates that I'm made up of. That brings me comfort because it also gives me a sense of identity with the community that I belong to.

And it helps me decide the kind of person I want to be. After working with these girls, I was so in love with one of them that I really wanted to adopt her. But, obviously, I wasn't an able candidate. But I knew at that point that I wanted to be a mom one day.'

P15's initial knowledge of who she is (that is, "I just knew that I wouldn't be able to live with myself if I had left them") forges the path for her deeper exploration of who she is and who she wants to become in the context of the particular group of people she "could not leave behind".

When she first goes to visit them, she does not know that she will connect with them or that they will connect with her so deeply. There can be little doubt that her original decision to visit would have been meaningful for her at the time, but as she experiences the actual visit, that meaning deepens and the significance of those initial encounters is enhanced. This is also a situation where philanthropic experience shapes personal experience (for example, wanting to be a mom one day).

In P15's sharing, we can observe all the key elements of significance.

- She vividly remembered these experiences of meaning.
- The memory of these vivid experiences continue into the longer term, not just weeks or months.
- The impact that these experiences of meaning have on shaping the choices she can make and the social environment she encounters is profound (that is, moving from San Francisco to Mexico).
- The impact that these vivid meaning experiences have on the way she thinks and feels in the here and now is also profound (for example, going from not wanting to be a mother to wanting to be a mother).
- These vivid meaning experiences have a significant impact on defining her sense of who she is.

We also note that the collective self that she cedes her singular self to provides her with a strong sense of what her essence and her collective's essence are. That collective essence is where she discovers how powerful her love as a mother could be.

## Conclusion

In this chapter, we have defined meaning and meaningfulness. We used the example of P13 to show that making sense of one's own life in the context of one's social context can be a very complex process and that the significance of these meanings in one's life can be enhanced over time. Sometimes, this enhancement is chosen by the individual, while other times it is not. In most cases, it is a combination of the two. The examples of P14 and P15 illustrate how meaning can be created and meaningfulness enhanced over time.

# 7

# Paths to meaningful philanthropy

Extant research exploring how people experience a sense of meaningfulness has primarily focused on the processes of developing belongingness, authenticity, transcendence, self-efficacy, self-worth/self-esteem and coherence (Rosso et al, 2010; King and Hicks, 2021).

We have already examined the role of belongingness, noting that many of our interviewees experience a deep sense of connection with the communities they care about. So deep is this sense of connection that they are willing to cede part of their identity and see themselves as part of those communities. As we have seen, that new perspective provides a rich source of additional meaning.

In this chapter, we focus on other paths to meaningful philanthropy. We begin with authenticity.

## Authenticity

Authenticity can be defined as a sense of alignment between one's behaviour and one's experience of the 'true' self (Sheldon et al, 1997). Authenticity is often described as a central underlying motive that helps individuals maintain a sense of meaning and order in their lives (Gecas, 1991).

When people's domain-specific experiences allow them to enact their sense of who they are or develop their knowledge of who they are (Spreitzer et al, 2005), they experience a higher degree of authenticity.

Regarding the elements of one's essential self that are known already, behaving consistently with one's interests, preferences and values can promote a deep sense of connection to that essential self (Sheldon and Elliott, 1998). For the elements of one's essential self that are still being discovered, experiencing the affirmation or verification of emerging qualities can help shape our understanding of who we are at our core (Gecas, 1991). In either scenario, the meaning of one's philanthropy is defined not only by the external impact created for others but also the degree to which the creation of such an impact can allow us to enact or develop our own sense of who we truly are. It is a well-documented phenomenon that our sense of self can provide an important source of meaning in our lives (Rosso et al, 2010).

In some situations, people experience these consistent or affirmational moments in a way that is more real and alive (Deci and Ryan, 1985). We might recall here the moments when P14 recognises the impact the ten-year-old soldier has had on her and when P15 wants to become a mother because of her experience with one of the girls she encountered on her journey.

The fact that there will always be unknowns in our true self or how those true self experience each moment does not seem to diminish the meaningfulness our interviewees are able to experience in different situations. Furthermore, with the passage of time, they come to recognise a new level of significance associated with these experiences – one that they did not know was possible before.

## Transcendence

Transcendence refers to the connecting or ceding of an individual's singular self to an entity greater than the singular or beyond the material world (Maslow, 1968). Psychologists have studied two types of transcendence (Madden and Bailey, 2019):

- *horizontal transcendence* – this explores situations in which people can make a connection with others they have relationships with – for example, colleagues, various organisational stakeholders and broader society;

- *vertical transcendence* – this connects people's daily activities to a divine entity or God figure.

Researchers have found that people experience a greater sense of meaningfulness in situations where transcendence is possible than in situations where it is not (Rosso et al, 2010). A second way in which transcendence has been studied is through a process called self-abnegation. This refers to how individuals deliberately subordinate themselves to something external to and/or bigger than the self. According to a self-abnegation perspective, transcending one's own self-interest by subordinating the singular self and relinquishing control to something greater provides individuals with a sense that they are not alone and that they do not need to be in control.

For example, an individual pursuing a sacred calling may experience meaningfulness by following and serving a higher power and having confidence that their destiny with that higher power will be fulfilled (Weiss et al, 2004). This may also be true for those who as followers of transformational leaders, are inspired to transcend the self to pursue shared goals. These processes are indeed experienced by many of our interviewees. Some do report a sense of transcendence, but as they explain, that transcendence can exhibit characteristics that they had not envisioned.

## Identity ceding and self-transcendence

Identity ceding is a special case of self-transcendence. We think it can deliver a heightened sense of meaningfulness beyond the vertical and horizontal transcendence outlined earlier. This is because this process maximises the chance that people can discover, experience or develop the dual alignments between their essential self and the communities they care about and achieve the outcomes desired by both. It provides one's essential self with affirmation from the external social reality.

Identity ceding does not require individuals to self-abnegate – at least not completely. If anything, it is a process in which individuals can develop their sense of self, not give it up. The only part of the self that is abnegated is the specific ceded object self. For every object self that is ceded, another object self, which is more effective in creating collective good, is developed. In addition, it is one's agentic self who is ceding one's object self. Hence, as one particular object self is ceded, the agentic self is developed into one more suited to create collective good with the community. The meta-self then monitors and guides the processes that the agentic self is following and facilitates closer alignment between that agentic self and one's essential self.

Our sample includes people from different religious or spiritual traditions. For the interviewees who have a spiritual practice, whether it is faith based or not, they have their own routines to experience transcendence consciously or subconsciously. What is shared between them is their commitment to utilising that vertical connection for the horizontal purpose of alleviation of human suffering or promotion of human potential. They are not necessarily aware of all the psychological processes that have supported them in making that connection, but they make the connection nevertheless. Equally, the presence of unknown elements in that process does not seem to reduce the meaningfulness they experience.

When they choose this greater horizontal entity to transcend themselves into, many choose to stretch their reach to the limits of their resources. These resources may be financial, intellectual, emotional, familial, social or spiritual. Such resources might also include knowledge of and conviction regarding who they truly are, especially before externally measurable successes can be created. In these situations, they allow their conviction to their essential self to guide their actions while overcoming pressures imposed externally. Sometimes, this effort may be applied for extended periods of time.

During that sometimes lengthy process, they experience the agency of holding on to what they believe to be the greater good that they are born to create. They also deploy that agency in the service of others. However, in contrast to self-abnegation or self-transcendence, they do not relinquish their control over the creation of the collective good. Nor do they passively connect with a focal community or relinquish *all* of who they are during the process. Rather, they actively engage with the purpose of creating a collective good, ceding only what is standing in the way of achieving that purpose and developing what can be helpful.

## The boundaries of self-transcendence: the case of P16

P16 described the boundaries of his self-transcendence. He said:

> 'I am at peace with myself in so far as I know I can't do everything, but the things I feel in our imperatives, I will do to the absolute best of my ability. I will make it the best of its kind in my domain in my country.
>
> I am doing my best in philanthropy, but that has to be in balance. It must not overtake my family, my health. Because, without those, you know, I'm not much good to any charitable organisation. Obviously, my family are the top priority for me, but if I filled my philanthropy meaningfully and productively, then good! Deep down, I am trying my hardest to do the best for my philanthropy.'

In assessing whether he has transcended the boundaries of self for the sake of the greater good, he uses the following yardstick: "deep down, I am trying my hardest to do the best for my philanthropy". His health and his family are the only boundaries that he places around his philanthropic activities, and even regarding these, he preserves his own health because it is the basis for his philanthropy.

## Identity ceding: implications for family relationships

In the selective transcendence for their philanthropy, our interviewees do not necessarily lose control of other aspects of their lives that are equally essential to their sense of who they are, such as their families. Many of them fully acknowledge that the environment in which they raise their families and the environment in which the community they help lives are not the same. They accept the reality that they cannot always expect their family members to transcend themselves in the same way that they do to care for the focal communities.

However, they do give the same care to their family that they give to the community. In caring for the community, they cede their own sense of self to the community they serve. If that community happens to be one their families also have an interest in, their job is very easy. They simply follow through with each other's shared interests.

Most often, however, the community that they personally choose to cede their self to is not the same community their family has an interest in. Equally, the way that they choose to practise their philanthropy is not necessarily the same way their families choose to practise theirs. The more they cede themselves to their community, the more difficult it can become for them to support their families' discovery of their own philanthropy when their families' choices are different from theirs.

Our interviewees have developed various strategies to cope with these conflicts.

- They choose to focus on specific domains or processes in which the potential for family conflict is minimised.
- They choose to mix and match what each family member owns. If someone owns the domain (what to do), others own the process (how to do it).
- They choose to explicitly allocate resources to serve the family's philanthropic interests but reserve enough to keep their own philanthropic interests alive.
- They create a portfolio of diversified philanthropic interests – one wide enough that it encompasses the opportunities that their family members need in order to discover their own philanthropic interests.
- They role-model their approach to path discovery for their family members and encourage them to explore their own philanthropic pathways independently.

We learned from our interviewees that families tend to focus their discussions about their family philanthropy on which domains and processes should form the focus, how they should maximise the impact of their resources, how they can address the concerns of their stakeholders and how they can uphold the family reputation in terms of both its heritage and its legacy.

As important as these topics are, they are superficial in comparison to:

- whether they take personal ownership of any of the domains or processes;
- how morally convicted they are about any given domains or processes;
- who they transcend themselves into and who they do not; and
- which elements of their object self they can cede to another, and which they cannot.

Failure to address these dimensions can result in making decisions that look good externally but which sacrifice the meaningfulness family members can ultimately experience from the process.

Very often, the root of conflict that families experience is not so much about the domains and processes of philanthropy, but rather which domains and processes family members experience as part of their essential self. Choosing one domain or process over another may involve choosing one family member's essential self over another's.

A more fruitful approach is not to ignore the essential self or which essential self family members choose to cede themselves to. Discussion can help reveal the deep-rooted sources of apparently superficial conflicts, help discover opportunities to acknowledge the deep ceding of identities that family members engage in to support one another's philanthropy, and then help explore the best domains and processes for the family, as a unit, to own. This way, their philanthropy can be most reflective of the essence of their family and their associated communities.

## Self-efficacy

Drawing boundaries between their life imperatives and choosing which identities to cede and which identities to develop is important for our interviewees, because it allows them to experience a sense of self-efficacy. Self-efficacy is the belief that one has the power and ability to produce an intended effect or make a difference (Bandura, 1977). When people experience a sense of personal autonomy in their activities, those activities become meaningful for them. All our interviewees have the kind of resources at their disposal that allow them to experience autonomy at a scale that is often unavailable to others. However, unless they set boundaries for the deployment of their resources, this autonomy can create stress and, eventually, burnout.

As an example, P16, for a period of his life, felt guilty because of his "inability to do everything". Given the resources he had, he would have liked to do more. He therefore developed a way of filtering what he pays attention to. He chooses to focus on what he can do instead of focusing on the demands that are placed on him. Most of our interviewees receive more requests for help than they can respond to, either as an individual, through their foundations or through their social circles. However, over time, through practice, some of them do find peace in terms of what they *can* do. Some of them also develop partnerships with organisations other than their own or become channels to other organisations to handle the overflow.

P16's illustration highlights the complexity of discovering this peace. What gives him his sense of self-efficacy is not just the fact that he is trying his hardest to do the best he can for his philanthropy but also the fact that he is doing his best in terms of all his life imperatives: his health, his family and his philanthropy. He has also discovered a way to make sense of what he cannot do outside of his imperatives – that is, believing that God will provide. In overcoming these challenges, although difficult, our interviewees could see themselves as learning, growing and effectively responding to challenges. As a result, they experience a greater sense of competence and effectiveness in what they do (Spreitzer et al, 2005).

When individuals feel they are making a difference or having a positive impact on others beyond the self, they feel more capable of affecting positive change, and thus they are more likely to experience greater levels of meaningfulness in what they do (Rosso et al, 2010). In reaching judgements about their self-efficacy, many of our interviewees cite the views of experts in their chosen field. P16's philanthropic success, for example, is recognised by leaders in his field and in his country to be trendsetting in his domain. Many others who we interviewed also collect evidence from domain experts to support their successes and seek constructive recommendations for their continued development.

Other interviewees without faith or spirituality define their life imperatives by what they can accomplish and choose not to let anything outside of that trouble them.

Drawing boundaries to protect one's experience of self-efficacy can become particularly challenging for individuals who have experienced trauma in their own lives due to, for example, child abuse or a collective tragedy, such as 9/11. It can be difficult to choose what they can and what they can't engage in without triggering that trauma. In those situations, they may seek to acquire boundary-setting skills, perhaps with professional support (for example, through career coaching, professional counselling or spiritual mentorship), and intentionally build a support structure to reinforce their boundaries. Providing a comprehensive set of techniques that people can use to deal with these situations is beyond the scope of this research, but it is a worthwhile area for further exploration.

Applying the knowledge and skills that one gains through personal experience in philanthropy and building deeply meaningful relationships that would not be possible without the philanthropic experience can both offer an additional source of meaning. They can enhance the meaningfulness people experience in their philanthropy because they help them realise the additional power and ability they have to affect meaningful change for others they care about. We have referred to P16's experience here, but there are many more examples in our data.

## Self-worth

Succeeding in something that we are doing and thus experiencing self-efficacy is not the same as feeling a sense of self-worth based on who we are (Baumeister, 1991). The former describes the feeling of accomplishment or affirmation resulting from one's actions, while the latter describes the feeling of being inherently valuable and worthy as a person regardless of what one achieves. In situations where people's sense of who they are is solely contingent on what they do, the two are not distinguishable. In most situations, however, people can experience a sense of inherent worth that is independent of what they do.

Next, we contrast the experiences of P16 with those of P17 to show the difference between self-worth and self-efficacy, and then we explore ways in which our interviewees experience the meaningfulness of their philanthropic actions through self-worth, drawing on the experiences of P18.

## Self-worth and self-efficacy: the case of P17

'I was asked recently, in a more business-oriented interview, about what ultimate success looks like, and I said that for me it looks like being able to sit at home in the sunshine and sort of just smile and stop and say I don't need to be validated anymore. I'm complete.'

What P17 explores here is the experience of self-worth. It is the inherent worth that he experiences as a person, without needing to be externally or internally validated. The path through which P17 attempts to achieve self-worth focuses on participation in an accumulation of activities that could increase his sense of self-efficacy. The process that P17 outlines is indeed one of the most documented processes for achieving a sense of self-worth (Spreitzer et al, 2005) – that is, creating successes and defining or redefining one's success as a person accordingly.

'But, until then, I will keep creating companies and keep driving forward in my philanthropy. And it doesn't feel like I am getting to the point where I will be complete. And even though I put that out there as – wouldn't that be an interesting state to get to – I don't feel anxious that I'm not getting there.

I'm comfortable receiving that feedback that then drives me forward to do the next thing. I'm very comfortable with the idea that for philanthropy to be sustainable, certainly for me and possibly for other people as well, it is entirely acceptable for there to be a feedback loop.

You know, some people have the view that philanthropy should be selfless, and you give it away and get nothing for it. You just do it because it is what it is, and I say: "Well, that may be fine for you, but for me, I quite like the people that I've helped to smile and say thank you." Because, then, I'm probably more likely to do it again, and it hasn't cost them anything to smile and say thank you, and I've appreciated receiving that, so that seems fine and that helps me keep moving forwards.

In fact, I'm sure there are things in my make-up as a human and in my early development, my early life, that lead me to want to receive positive feedback in order to keep driving me forwards. Partly in order to prove that I am in some sense worthy and that I belong and that I'm worthy, and you, whoever you are, are happy for me to be here. It may even be a sort of protection mechanism. I do things that ensure that people I interact with are happy that I'm there on the basis that maybe if they stop being happy that I'm there, they'll tell me to go away somewhere, and wouldn't that be terrible.

I'm [also] very comfortable with people going off and not remembering that I was involved in any way. I still receive the feedback in a sense. If I see someone that I've helped ... the young women at the school, some of them know that I exist and that I created the school and all the rest of it, but some of them don't really know. When I went along to the non-profit organisation I created, to its tenth anniversary, there were loads of people there who had no idea who I was, and in fact I don't really know who they were either, and yet being there and seeing it all and seeing them scurrying about and wearing their uniforms and getting places at universities and this, that and the other, I still smile to myself and think I did this. This didn't exist until I sketched it on a napkin and I brought it to life. Isn't that cool. I don't actually need them to give me that feedback. I just need to know that I did that and I put that in the world. Isn't that good? So, I think that's the way I relate to it.'

P17 notes that despite receiving consistently positive feedback on self-efficacy through his various activities, his self-worth is elevated further through the knowledge that he has made a positive contribution to the community.

Others in our sample note that their self-efficacy, self-worth or even to some extent their essential self are not relevant to their philanthropic decisions. They may already have ceded their singular self for the alleviation of some collective suffering or the flourishing of some collective potential. When that ceding occurs, the meaning achieved through impact can be joint or shared, but so too can a sense of self-worth. If the community experiences a heightened sense of self-worth, so too can the philanthropist. We do not have a large enough sample to be truly emphatic about the philanthropist's path to meaningfulness. However, most of our interviewees seem to function in a space in which their sense of self-worth and self-efficacy do play a part in shaping their philanthropy.

## Inherited wealth and self-worth: the case of P18

P18 experiences her self-worth in a different way. Many second-generation or multigeneration wealth inheritors have their own challenges to overcome when finding what is personally meaningful for them in philanthropy. Individuals in our sample evaluate their self-efficacy by assessing what they themselves could achieve, not what their family wealth could achieve. However, their evaluation of their self-efficacy cannot necessarily be experienced in isolation from who they are born to be – that is, someone who inherits wealth. Making sense of this essential element of who they are and experiencing a sense of worth associated with it can be challenging. P18's reflection highlights this complexity.

'In particular, there was this amazing woman of colour who runs a Black feminist domestic violence organisation, and I started off by saying: "Philanthropy and most of the wealth that is being redistributed or that you're applying for funding from has come through harmful practices that have exploited people of colour, and I just want to repair that by having a relationship with you and building trust with you and supporting you with resources and in any other ways that we can."

And she started crying because she just felt shock. She's like: "I've never heard of a White person ever mentioning reparations before and taking at least some responsibility or at least acknowledging the systems that have caused this harm." And then I started crying, and I do think there was a beautiful connection between us ... that was much more grounded in love.

And, you know, I hope that we can build alternatives and that we can repair and I can repair as well. I don't have to hold this responsibility and guilt and shame on my own. There are ways to slowly and beautifully be part of building something different or trying to do something different. So that was powerful, but that's just one example, and I think I'm still on that journey.'

In this case, P18 may experience self-efficacy because she succeeds in creating a genuine connection with the CEO. That connection is meaningful for them both, and the fact that she provides the CEO with an opportunity to have the injustice she has experienced acknowledged is significant.

That, however, is not the same as P18 feeling a sense of self-worth because of who she is or who she was born to be. P18 still experiences a sense of personal shame associated with how the wealth she and her family possess was created. Her self-worth is still tainted by the power she holds in terms of her wealth. When asked if she could think of a moment when she could practise her philanthropy completely free of that sense of shame, she said:

'No, I cannot. Unfortunately, I don't think completely free is possible ... I have not gotten there yet. I think, ultimately, I'm still making decisions and I'm holding a lot of power. The way that we practise our philanthropy is pretty complicated.

I mentioned earlier an organisation that I really admire and believe in around participatory grant making, and they kind of democratise how decisions get made over where funding goes.

But the majority of our grants are still being held by a board of White people with privilege, with a lot of class privilege, and who have very little lived experience of the direct injustices. Not a 100 per cent disconnection, but we're still making a lot of decisions with a lot of power. I think, because of that, I have not felt fully liberated from that anger and disgust towards that target [the system of injustice], and I'm not sure I ever will. Or maybe I will. I'm just not sure.'

Then, P18 was asked if she could think of a moment when she could feel as free as possible from that sense of shame. She said:

'Probably not in a philanthropic setting ... because there's still this kind of, like, saviour mentality, even in that conversation. When I think about it, I shiver a little bit, because I was still the person with the money that was saying: "This is to repair harm." And she was like: "That's really unusual for somebody in your position to take this approach." But it was still ultimately me giving something and that didn't feel like solidarity, and I think solidarity has to feel different.

And, for me, when I've been in more activist spaces, where I have felt really committed to whatever issue we were fighting for, whether it was to make it safer for women on college campuses from challenging rape culture or fighting to get our university to divest from the fossil fuel industry, which is what I did when I was in college, I remember feeling like super in alignment and in solidarity with the people I was fighting with and in struggle with. I guess maybe those are the moments that I felt more liberated.'

The difference between P17 and P18 lies in how they define themselves. During the interview, P17 shares how, at least in part, he defines who he is by what he can achieve. When he then achieves something, his self-worth is affirmed through his increased sense of self-efficacy. P18 defines who she is by what she possesses (because that is what she was born into) as well as by who she would be without her wealth and what she can achieve as an individual without wealth.

P18 experiences a higher self-worth from the part of her that is not associated with her wealth than the part that is. She experiences a strong sense of solidarity and liberation when she connects with others (that is, the CEO and other activists) through the part of her that she deems more worthy (that is, being an activist). That solidarity and liberation then makes the experience more meaningful for her.

## Coherence

Coherence captures humans' need to understand and make sense of their lives and the world more broadly (Heintzelman and King, 2014). This innate curiosity is directed both outwardly and inwardly. At its most basic level, coherence arises when one understands experience – when a person feels they 'get it' (Hicks et al, 2010). We might recall the moment when P12 utters the words "*important but underappreciated photographers*" and when P8 recognises that the memory of the bird on the tree sticks with him but the detail of the sale of his businesses does not.

This 'getting it' is not just a question of understanding what happens externally but also knowing how people, ideas, objects and other things are connected (Heine et al, 2006). When people can find that connection and experience a sense of belonging though that understanding, life makes more sense (Baumeister and Vohs, 2002) and they experience more coherence. As coherence develops, people feel that, overall, their life is more meaningful. This sense of coherence is usually experienced in people's life as a whole, across their personal life, their professional life and their philanthropy. We illustrated a life with a high level of coherence with the example of P13. When he defines who he is by who 'we' are, all the elements of his life fall into place. Next, we provide a further illustration drawing on the experience of P19.

### Identity coherence: the case of P19

P19's reflection is illustrative of the coherence that our interviewees experience in different aspects of their life. As P19 reflects, he considers himself lucky that his business identity happens to lie at the essence of who he is. That alone, however, does not make up his holistic sense of his essential self.

'I am who I am, but I am essentially what I have done. And, hopefully, what I've done is trust building. I've done other things in my life, but I am the sum of what I have lived through. Can I put aside everything I've done and say there is someone else there that exists independent of what I have done. I cannot give you that answer. If you have done something professionally that truly expressed you in the self, then it's one [and] the same. A lot of people certainly do not get to do something professionally that expresses their inner self, in which case they would tell you: "I have my private life, and I have my professional life." I ... for better or worse, there is no difference for me between the private and the professional.

The pure philanthropy activities I described to you are as much part of my self as what I've done professionally. I don't see it as compartments of my life. I see they are as one in the self.

What I do in the world of finance ... my philanthropic activities stem from it and come from the same desire to say, in my professional life, in my professional universe, I can improve the environment in such a way as to improve the fate of clients. The organisation I built can improve fairness. I can improve transparency. I can improve the service, you know, all kinds of things which are important and where the financial performance of clients would be better if you do that.

It's just important from the moral standpoint, and it's important from a contribution standpoint. I mean, we don't spend a lot of time on this ... this planet. So in the grand scheme of things, you would really want to leave it a better place when you go. And, hopefully, you can use your professional life to leave it a better place, and I did that in my field.

I'm very aware that I'm not Dr Martin Luther King, so I am cognisant that changing the world has different meanings for different people, but at my scale, I feel that, professionally speaking, I have made a very positive contribution to my field.

When I look at what we I've done in a pure philanthropic domain, I don't see it as radically different. I am improving the world there as well. They are different fields, but there is a kind of common thread between what I do professionally and what I do in my philanthropy.'

He went on to describe his contributions using the metaphor of an impressionist painting:

'From a distance, you get a sense of the holistic image that is being conveyed, but as you get close up, you realise that some of the dots are supplied by philanthropy and some are supplied by business. I've had the good fortune of marrying both the personal and the professional, and there is a certain logic in the general colours that you get out of my painting.

I wouldn't pick any of the dots to describe who I am. You know, you have to see all of them to see the full personality. They go together.

But I have something else to tell you. One of the key things I've learned – one of the common features of the financial part is that the painting is never finished, so that sense of wholeness that you are alluding to never fully happens. Maybe, at the end of life, we can feel we are full and have completion.

I'm speaking for myself, but I think it's the case for many entrepreneurs. You feel that you're never quite satisfied with where you got to. You feel that there is so much more to be done in all aspects really. That sense of not being satisfied is what keeps you going.'

P19 is right. This is shared by everyone in our sample. Nobody feels as though they have experienced a sense of completion, and all of them want to keep going.

*Experiencing coherence: the case of P20 and P21*

P20's experiences show a very different way of experiencing coherence. He focuses on coherence in the sense of always persevering despite challenges.

'The hardest part of that threshold to become a leader is those critical moments where, right before the negative shifted into positive, the person chose not to give up. Yes, the whole key of life is successfully managing pain – both the pain for yourself and the pain visited upon you by others.'

He had experienced a period of homelessness, and was asked if there had been a moment when he thought he wouldn't make it.

'It's not a moment. I know you keep asking the question, looking for that set day and time. It doesn't work like that because, for me, every day was Groundhog Day. Every day, to function, I had to hide, hide my homelessness. Every day, I had to hide the car I was using because my plates were out of date. Every day, I had to look out for the police. Every day, I had to put a cover over the car. It was just simply surviving. It was surviving through that process and coming out on the other side better than I went into it.

I was running an office with the $500 of rent money. That's the reason I was homeless. I took the money I was using to pay rent for a home and used it instead as a rent payment for an office, so I could work. I was working in that office late enough so that when the people left, I could then go into the bathroom and take a wash in the basin of the washroom. And I was washing my arms and neck and then washing my shirt and getting the stains off of it and washing my shoes, and that was de-dignifying and inspiring in the same breath. I had not given up.'

In what P20 describes, coherence is experienced in how he defines who he is (that is, someone who does not give up) in this social context. This coherence is not experienced only after the conclusion of homelessness, but rather in every moment he experienced both humiliation and inspiration simultaneously.

A similar way of experiencing coherence can also be seen as P20 explains his general approach to his philanthropy and how it shapes his attitudes towards others. Growing up, P20 had experienced the personal hardship, poverty and violence that is created by racial injustice. His non-profit organisation exists to create an economic infrastructure for disadvantaged people in his society. This is how he describes what he does:

> 'What we got to find is this more balanced system where you take smart government, smart taxation to create free enterprises and opportunity for all. Anybody willing to work hard and play by the rules and do for themselves. We're creating economic infrastructure for the bottom 50 per cent of society.
>
> And for Black America, creating an economic infrastructure that has never existed ever in this country. For Black Americans, we have a sports infrastructure. We have a civil rights infrastructure. We've got a racism infrastructure. We have got a political infrastructure. We don't have an economic and financial infrastructure. That's my mission in my life: creat[ing] this infrastructure and putting this in place so that you can have social justice through an economic lens.
>
> I'm trying to update social justice to the 21st century so that everybody, including the worst racist on the planet, who just wants to make more money, I mean, says: "Okay, I don't really like Black people per se, but I'll do it anyway because it benefits me." ... What I try to do is creat[e] a system that no matter how backwards you might be, you don't kick me out of your office.'

His non-profit organisation exists to create an economic infrastructure for the most disadvantaged people in his society. His reaction to the injustice he has suffered is not to right the particular wrong he personally experienced, but rather to find a solution that can help all others who could potentially be subject to injustice in the same way. He does not differentiate the people he helps based on the colour of their skin (that is, the source of the social injustice he experienced), but based on their economic position.

It is at this point in the interview that he was asked about how he defines 'love' and what he thinks about the intention behind giving. He was asked whether the 'yes' he gets from a racist to do the right thing for economic reasons is love. He offered the following:

> 'Love is work. ... My job is to do the work. That's my job ... and to get that job done ... I'm going to love you, whether you're loving or not.
>
> I'll put it another way. If you want to have a little grace, you better show a little mercy.
>
> Mercy is when some ranting son of a bitch does not get the rear-end whipping he deserves because he's a racist. I don't mean literally a whipping. I mean psychologically, intellectually, spiritually. He doesn't get the whipping he so rightly deserves because he's a racist, because he's whatever. ... That's mercy.
>
> But grace is when you and I get the blessings and the gifts that we don't deserve. I believe the universe has a perfect accounting system. Whatever goes around comes around.
>
> So if you want to have a little grace, you should show a little mercy. So I try to talk without being offensive, listen without being defensive, and you always leave even your adversary with their dignity because, if you don't, they spend the rest of their life trying to make you miserable. It becomes personal, and so, at some point, you got to forgive.'

P20 experiences his coherence in his external environment not by changing others' minds and assimilating them to his point of view, but rather by ceding the essence of his identity – in this case an individual who has experienced racial injustice – to the greater good he wants to create: a social justice system for the 21st century. In order to achieve this, not only does he cede his identity of being a survivor of social injustice to the greater community that he serves (that is, the economically disadvantaged), but he cedes the same identity to the racists he encounters by working on an economic solution that is acceptable to them. In doing so, he does not, in any sense, compromise his moral values; rather, he applies the same moral conviction to live out what is right for him: forgiveness.

This way of operating is not unique to the interviewees who have a faith background. P21 articulated a similar personal philosophy before he made it clear that he does not have any faith. His way of mobilising resources in order to create change is to meet the selfish needs of each individual to create collective good. In his words, "collective selfishness can be selflessness" when organised for the right purpose. Both P20 and P21 cede their identities, which are based on caring for their community, to their peer groups, who do not care in the same way. In doing so, they experience coherence between both what they choose to do and how they choose to care as well as what others choose to do and how they choose to care. P20 continued as follows:

'The result of [my way of working] is that they would unleash resources that allow other people to express love for themselves and love for America and love for opportunity and love for free enterprise and love for potential, so they're showing up.

I showed love. The other people that are gonna get help show love. And, hopefully, as a result of that, this person whose thinking is backwards might see that they have been on the wrong side of history and, possibly, the wrong side of the definition of love, because now they're getting appreciation that they don't really deserve. They're getting a legacy they don't really deserve. And ultimately, they get hooked on the drug of authenticity and begin to become less about me and more about we.'

Many scholars have explored the question of whether negative and, sometimes, extremely negative events are necessary in order for people to discover meaning and experience meaningfulness. Some suggest that negative experiences can serve to boost meaning because they stimulate comprehension (Vohs et al, 2019). That is, people are challenged to understand how the event fits into a broader narrative of the self, relationships and the world. Others suggest that positive feelings are more conducive to helping broaden mindsets and build up personal and relational resources in order to generate greater good (Fredrickson, 2001). Still others suggest that positive events could reinforce expectations of stability and order in the world around us, which then reinforces our sense of coherence. Meanwhile, negative events force us to confront our ideas about what is truly meaningful and arrive at a level of coherent understanding of ourselves and the world that is not otherwise possible.

In a qualitative study of this nature, we cannot draw causal conclusions about whether positive or negative events can generate more meaningfulness in philanthropy or people's lives. What we can see, however, is how meaning and meaningfulness can be created through coherence created with both negative and positive experiences.

At least one third of our interviewees have survived some form of trauma. This includes trauma related to personal health, family health, systemic social injustice, individual or collective displacement, and collective trauma, such as that created by 9/ 11. All of them have discovered their ways of turning negatives into positives, and most of them are using the personal and collective resources they have built in order to overcome negatives in their own lives for the purpose of creating greater good for their communities. The coherence offered by this narrative, we think, can be more meaningful than coherence based solely on making sense of one's personal experiences in one's own personal circumstances.

## Conclusion

In this chapter, we reviewed the various paths that lead to a more meaningful philanthropic experience. Although all these paths were primarily explored in the context of philanthropy, people can experience meaningfulness in these ways in all aspects of their lives.

All the paths we explored can thus enhance the meaningfulness of not only one's philanthropic experience but also one's personal and professional experiences. We thus illustrated these paths with examples from all facets of life, and showed how they form a coherent whole with people's philanthropic journey.

# 8

# Conclusion

For us, one of the key takeaways from this research is just how much the 'self' is at the root of philanthropy. While 20th-century notions of the dichotomy of altruism versus self-interest have pervaded much of the current debate about the role of philanthropists in society, our research indicates that this is too shallow a perspective. It is the presence of the self in a psychological sense, not its absence, that shapes meaning and encourages philanthropy.

Philanthropy has been criticised for imposing solutions on (particularly developing) communities and giving primacy to the needs of donors. Our research provides new evidence regarding why such an approach may be misguided. However, rather than focusing entirely on communities and diverting attention from donor needs, our research suggests that it may be more fruitful to develop a concomitant focus on donors and the person behind the giving.

Our notion of identity ceding is new to the literature and critical to this debate. We have shown that as donors reflect more deeply on the nature of their selves and what is meaningful for those selves, they are drawn more closely to the communities they care about. At that point, they can experience a willingness to cede part of who they are to that community. As that happens and they experience oneness with the community, the dichotomy between donor needs and community needs no longer has meaning. They become one and the same. Thus, in seeking to develop philanthropy that is more aligned with the needs of marginalised communities, it can be helpful to encourage philanthropists to reflect on the nature of their true self and what might be most meaningful for that self. Decisions can then be made about what can be ceded to become one with the community.

It is important to note here that none of our interviewees frame this process as a loss (that is, as giving something away). They all see it as opening the door to a richer and deeper sense of meaning. Thus, it will be helpful to encourage philanthropists to iterate the process of meaning exploration that we describe in this text. Sources of meaning they do not anticipate will very likely emerge.

We identified in our research that one of the richest sources of meaning for philanthropists is the deep sense of connection and closeness they develop with communities through their philanthropy. The experience of a shared relational identity, in particular, opens the door to understanding what is meaningful for the focal community as well as for the philanthropist themself. The content and direction of philanthropy can then be guided accordingly. However, critically, so too can the nature of the philanthropist's journey of self-discovery and growth. As richer sources of meaning and meaningfulness are experienced, the greater the likelihood that that the individual's philanthropy can make a deep and lasting difference in their search for a meaningful life. We see this as a scenario in which both the donor and the community can gain, and gain substantively.

## The role of the unknown

For us, the most unexpected finding from our research was the role of the unknown in people's reflections. Not only does the unknown not prevent people from carrying out philanthropic activities, but it can become the very fuel that drives them forward. Simply stated, they can seek out philanthropy as a vehicle for discovering more about who they are and what impact they can create. The nature of the unknown and how it contributes to meaningfulness can be summarised as follows.

- Interviewees accept that there is and will always be a level of unknown in their understanding of their social environment, themselves and their essential self.
- The unknown does not stop them from experiencing who they are, acting on this knowledge or continuing to learn more about

what is unknown about themselves. Some of them explicitly integrate what is unknown into part of who they are in their essence, and everything they do then is afforded a degree of freedom to accommodate that unknown.

- Similarly, the unknown does not alter their beliefs about the essence of who they are. They allow their beliefs to guide their actions in the absence of externally available feedback until such feedback becomes available. Sometimes, they may need to proceed on the basis of their beliefs for many years before the unknown can be replaced by some form of external confirmation.

- What people do not know about the meaning or meaningfulness of their philanthropy does not reduce the meaning and meaningfulness associated with what they do know. What is known about their meaning and meaningfulness can change and deepen, even when people are unaware of the process taking place. Not being able to predict the trajectory of this change does not prevent it from happening.

- Unknowns can also occur with respect to the impact one's initiatives have on a focal community. Unknowns associated with what will happen if one fails in one's actions to help others may provoke anxiety and stress. That stress may be reduced if people believe that a greater power will take care of things or that their trying, in and of itself, has inherent meaning. Stress can also be reduced if people develop rules for managing their philanthropy stipulating that they will not let factors outside of their control bother them. In some situations, this type of unknown can directly affect how people experience meaningfulness.

## The importance of reflection

It is important for us to recognise that because our interviewees' primary attention is focused on the collective good they can create for others through their philanthropy, not all of them invest time in thinking about what is personally meaningful for them during that journey. We found only a few, for example, reflecting on how they define themselves and which part of them is creating the achievement, using the language we have provided here. However, in their discussion, they routinely reference their sense of who they are. There is always a role that their experiential agentic self plays. They refer to this sense of self by making statements such as 'I choose to own this process' or 'I know I do not feel comfortable about this kind of philanthropy'. Their experiential agentic self is always playing the role of a knower and a chooser, without necessarily being explicitly labelled as such.

Some of our interviewees even said, explicitly, that in their philanthropy they never think about themselves; they think only about others. But even in these situations, their experiential agentic self is still choosing – choosing to not think about themselves and choosing to only think about others. They still have a sense of self as they think about their philanthropy.

If we can help people identify the elements of self that are making choices, we may have a way to help them experience a higher level of self-worth in their philanthropy through alignment with the essential self. In doing so, family members for whom the essential self matters can be encouraged to truly integrate it into their philanthropy. Family members for whom the essential self isn't relevant in a particular domain/process can support other family members in their choices without sacrificing anything. This higher clarity in respect of the match between people's essential self and their philanthropy increases the chance that all family members can find the philanthropy that is truly theirs.

Another benefit that people can experience through this type of internal reflection is that they can get in touch with the meta-self. Challenges can present themselves in many philanthropic initiatives. They may be practical and project related, or they may be derived from issues with a multiplicity of relationships. Overcoming these challenges often requires the management not only of external conflict but also internal conflict between different elements of our sense of self. The meta-self is the one element of our self that specialises in managing such conflict. Reflecting on its role in the journey of philanthropy can be beneficial because most of our identities are constructed in facets of our lives not associated with philanthropy. Since the meta-self that we engage in our philanthropy can cross-fertilise conflict resolution in other aspects of our lives, it can contribute to our psychological wellbeing and the meaningfulness we experience in life.

## An understandable reluctance

The learning we have outlined has profound implications not only for philanthropists and the communities they serve, but also for the professions that facilitate the philanthropic process – notably philanthropic advisors and fundraisers. In this text, we have suggested a multitude of ways that the experience of philanthropy can be deepened, identifying new sources of meaning and meaningfulness that can be experienced and explored. Conversations about these topics can also allow donors to explore connections with various aspects of self, notably the essential self.

Despite the obvious utility of learning from the experiences of others, we anticipate that there may still be some reluctance on the part of some fundraisers and advisors to engage in these kinds of conversations. The hesitation to engage in this way can originate from the fear that the conversation will get too personal and intrude on the donors' privacy. They may also worry that they don't yet have the kind of deeply trusting relationships that are necessary to host this kind of discussion. Yet a failure to engage in this way can deprive a philanthropist of substantive meaning and thus impact their ability to sustain and develop their philanthropy. So the solution should not be to avoid having the potentially deeply transformative conversations, but rather to learn the knowledge and practise the skills necessary to understand and support the journey that philanthropists undertake. Advisors should also recognise that it isn't necessary to have all the answers from the outset. They can become comfortable in navigating the unknown with their clients and recognising the value of the unknown as a potential source of meaning and psychological wellbeing. This is an important point, since advisors are often hired to reduce unknowns rather than nurture them.

Most of the time, why people start their philanthropy and what they find meaningful after they begin their journey is not the same. So an overemphasis on the impact of philanthropy from the outset is, in our view, unhelpful, as it potentially stifles additional sources of meaning that can be created for all parties. While it is intuitive that philanthropists care for others, there is no reason that they should not care for themselves on their journey, if only to ensure that the journey is sustainable and headed to the 'right' destination for the community. We also learned that the outside perception of community needs is often out of alignment with what the community itself feels it needs. Having the sensitivity to listen and adjust one's initial philanthropic intent is therefore important. This was intuitive for most of our interviewees. What wasn't so intuitive, however, was that our philanthropists were willing to morph not only their actions or approach, but also who they were into who their community needed them to be. The process of transformation could be deeply meaningful in and of itself, but it also allowed our philanthropists to experience any gains for the community as part of that community, accentuating the psychological wellbeing and feelings of self-worth that could result.

## Key findings

Other key learning that emerged from our research provides answers to the following questions, which can help people reflect on their own philanthropy.

1. Why do HNWIs and UHNWIs choose to begin a philanthropic journey?
   Most of our interviewees start their philanthropic journey with a search for impact. They want to do the most good with the limited resources they have. These resources include financial resources but also time, talent, energy, social networks and influence.
   Few people start their philanthropic journey with an explicit search for meaning. When they do, it is typically in response to an unexpected surge in wealth or a windfall that could not be redistributed based on existing patterns of thought. They then need to redefine the purpose that philanthropy could fulfil in their lives.
   Only very occasionally did we find interviewees who start their philanthropic journey knowing that during this process they

would both discover what impact they were capable of and evolve their sense of who they are. Those who do are often individuals who have experienced individual or collective trauma, which has led them to a higher level of self-reflection. Overall, people rarely start and sustain their philanthropic journey with the same understanding about what is meaningful for them. We did not have a single interviewee who told us that they began their philanthropic journey in search of a community that they could become one with or that they were about to embark on a deeply transformative journey of experiencing love and compassion with. Many, however, see these as their most meaningful experiences after having been on their journey in philanthropy for many years.

2. How do philanthropic activities become owned by HNWIs and UHNWIs, and why?

For people who have had no philanthropic experience of their own, but grew up with a family tradition of philanthropy, taking ownership of their philanthropy might require that they differentiate the part of their philanthropy that is reflective of their family's tradition from the part that is reflective of their unique sense of self. People who have accumulated their own wealth (and hence have the freedom to establish their own traditions) can reflect on how taking ownership of their wealth accumulation journey relates to how they take ownership in their philanthropy.

In their wealth accumulation journey, some people experience ownership of the domains and processes they adopt, while others do so to a lesser extent. Those who have experienced ownership in their wealth accumulation journey tend to anchor their ownership of philanthropy on those previous experiences. Those who haven't experienced ownership in their wealth accumulation journey tend to anchor their philanthropic experience on other facets of their lives where ownership has been experienced. There are still others who have yet to decide what to own in their lives. For them, their philanthropic experience can become a continuation of their search for ownership.

When people do take ownership of their philanthropy, it could be their personal identity that is taking ownership (for example,

'I do this type of philanthropy because I am an innovative entrepreneur who has expertise in solving this particular kind of problem'), their collective identity that is taking ownership (for example, 'I am part of the community that my business operates in, and my community needs my help') or their moral identity that is taking ownership (for example, 'this is my way of being kind, not my family's'). It could also be a combination of any of these. When these identities take ownership of people's philanthropy, both the process of taking ownership and the ownership claimed over certain philanthropic activities help philanthropists make sense of why they do what they do and hence how they can experience meaning in their choices.

The meaning they can derive from their philanthropic choices is hence a function of how meaningfully they can experience the identities who are taking ownership. The identities who are taking on new layers of meaning through their decisions to take ownership and the fact of ownership itself can both provide meaning. That one may experience meaning in the latter way is intuitive. That one may experience meaning in the former is not. Family philanthropy can also provide a rich sense of meaning. This is because individuals make their philanthropic decisions in the context of their parents', their grandparents' and other family members' decisions. If any of these others take psychological ownership over these decisions, the dialogue between the singular selves becomes a dialogue between collective selves in a family unit. The essence of the meaning that derives from this discussion can then become very complex very quickly. Of course, family members can take ownership of not only their philanthropy but also the domains and processes they have used to accumulate (and to continue to accumulate) their wealth. There may be situations where the relationships the family experiences with their wealth accumulation community are not compatible with the relationships the family experiences with their philanthropic community. Deep reflection, both singularly and collectively, will need to be carried out to help the individual, the family unit and the community they help to reach a shared understanding about what goals they want to achieve together and why.

3. What are the underlying principles that steer the selection of what to own and what not to?

Most often, what guides the selection of what to own and what not to own in one's philanthropy is how much the selection is reflective of the dual alignment between the essence of the philanthropist and the essence of the community they want to help. The exact same impact created for exactly the same community may create meaning for some philanthropists but not others. Equally, particular domains and processes may hold appeal for some philanthropists and not others. Ownership decisions are typically driven by a sense of fit.

In many cases, the essence of the community is articulated by the community itself. Clearly, they know their own essence better than others do, so philanthropists need to choose to listen to them. In rare cases, the essence of the community is articulated by the philanthropist because they are the only person who has viewed the community through a particular lens. In most cases in our research, however, our philanthropists have to tap into community knowledge to properly distil the essence. Often, they do so by forging relationships with key individuals so that together they can create a new social reality, a new set of social norms and, hence, a new articulation of the collective essence, as shaped by the transformation.

Meaning, especially in the latter scenario, can be experienced by both the resultant shape of philanthropy and the process through which that shape emerges. The more this process can help philanthropists affirm what they know already about who they are in their essence, the more this process can provide them with meaning. Equally, the more this process can help philanthropists discover what they do *not* know about themselves, the more this process can provide them with meaning.

4. Do philanthropists need to be willing to morph their sense of self during their philanthropic journey?

If the desire is to maximise the impact on the community, the short answer here is yes. In the philanthropic journeys that create the richest meaning for our philanthropists, their sense of self is typically transformed during the process. In particular, it is transformed in a way that allows them to experience the creation of a new social reality by becoming part of their focal community.

This transformation does not require that they become capable of fully empathizing with the community, experiencing what they experience. Nor does it imply that they have relinquished control of all their resources to the community. Rather, this means they develop a sense of agentic self and meta-self that willingly allows their objective selves to be morphed by the community. The resultant self can then be more effective in achieving shared goals.

The ceding of identities was rarely described by interviewees as sacrifice. Rather, they observed clear benefits from the self-transformation process. Their agentic selves become better at knowing which labels they should use to describe who they are and better at understanding how these labels should be defined in order to best practise their philanthropy. Similarly, their meta-self becomes better at managing any conflicts that their agentic selves experience, even when such conflicts might be experienced across different aspects of their life, such as in their philanthropic life, their business life and their personal life. The self-worth and self-efficacy that they experience through their meta-self and agentic selves and through their emergent object selves far outweighs the loss of selected object selves.

The ceding process is rarely experienced as a thought exercise only. Transformations are often emotionally charged. Philanthropists learn to empathise with the community and where this is not possible, grow their sense of compassion toward them. Both the thought process of their self-transformation and the associated compassion they experience can create meaning in their lives. These can form a part of their understanding about who they are as a person and let them live that out in other aspects of their lives beyond philanthropy.

5. Is giving for the self or selfless?

   In a sense, we have already addressed this in the opening to this chapter. A wide range of views were articulated by our philanthropists. Some rely on what they can do for the community to define who they are. They consider the relationship one of dependence. They depend on the community to define their sense of self and the meaning they are able to derive from it. At the other extreme, some interviewees told us that everything they do in their philanthropy is about others, and nothing is about them per se. Of course, a hybrid experience is also evident, where people compartmentalise the part of themselves that can be defined by the needs of others and select a portion of their philanthropy that can be deeply personally meaningful.

In all of these cases, people's agentic self experiences the meaning of their lives through their choice of how they define their sense of self. Even in the most extreme situations where people say what they do has nothing to do with them and everything to do with the community, their agentic self still chooses to define who they are in that way. People still make a statement about who they are in the context of their philanthropy and ascribe significant meaning to their lives as a consequence.

None of our interviewees said that they have reached a state of completeness or wholeness in their understanding of who they are or what they can achieve. All of them, when asked, said they are looking for more. They are looking for more that they can create for others, and they are looking for more in the sense of who they can be or become. Embracing the unknown seems to be driving them on in terms of sustaining their philanthropy. The unknown does not deter them from pursuing philanthropy or taking actions. Similarly, the richness of meaning that they can experience during their journey of seeking greater impact does not seem to be reduced by the presence of unknowns.

6. How do philanthropists sustain their journey?

The more obvious answer to what sustains their philanthropy is the achievement of impact or the hope that one day their desired impact will be achieved. The less obvious answer is to experience rewarding friendships and create an environment through which creative solutions are more likely to emerge. But these are not the only ways through which people's philanthropy can be sustained.

We found that the process that people go through in order to clarify what their desirable impact should be could be sustaining in and of itself, because they find meaning in their pursuit.

The experience of standing in the gap in the face of a series of disappointments, or the deep disappointment experienced when certain impact cannot be made, can offer as much meaning as seeing a really challenging goal finally achieved. This is especially the case when standing in the gap defines who they are, and the essence of who they are is rooted in the community they care about.

These sources of sustainability do not necessarily rely on receiving external feedback. To the contrary, it is when the external environment is extremely challenging and the lack of external feedback continues to be frustrating that people can experience this source of sustainability. It provides individuals with an alternative source of meaning as they navigate the complexity of the problem they face, carry on doing what they do and experiment with how to source the information necessary to achieve clarity over the achievement of impact.

Without this internal source of sustainability, we think, philanthropists run the risk of being pressurised to focus on high-impact philanthropy that can crowd out the kind of philanthropy capable of maximising meaning both for the philanthropists themselves and the communities they care about. The solution to reducing this risk, however, is not to push back against the current trend and deemphasise impact. Rather, it is to build up the often ignored or underappreciated muscles associated with alternative sources of meaning. We hope that the search for meaning can be at least as important as the search for impact and that the two may be considered concurrently.

7. What factors shape the meaning of philanthropy and how meaningful the experience can be?

The most significant learning that we gained about meaning in this research is that it can be experienced beyond the impact that philanthropy can achieve. Meaning can be experienced during the process of clarifying what impact is desirable and creating a new social reality through which the impact can emerge. The emerging description of impact will be more reflective of not only the essence of the community but also, as we noted earlier, the philanthropists' essence of who they are. This is because the philanthropist takes the time to morph themselves in order to listen as a part of the community.

Both the process of working out the impact and the process of making sense of the impact in the context of one's own sense of self can provide meaning. While the latter reflection may sound superficially 'self-centred', this self-centring is carried out for a collective good. At the most straightforward level, this reflection can itself be a source of meaning that can help sustain one's philanthropic efforts. It provides both the philanthropist and the community more time to work on solutions. Less obviously, this reflection can provide the philanthropist with a more prescriptive map about which part of themselves they need to cede to the community, allowing them to contribute best to the achievement of their shared goal.

This self-reflection helps transform what seems, on the surface, to be an external conflict between what a philanthropist wants to achieve and what it is possible to achieve in a social environment into an internal conflict between what a philanthropist can or cannot cede in order to maximise the collective good. The philanthropist has much more control over the resolution of the internal conflict than the external one. If they can discover internal solutions that are under their control, they will be in a much better position to navigate the external environment for the discovery of community solutions.

As we noted earlier, undertaking such reflections and choosing which part of one's object self to cede to the community was not described as self-sacrifice by any of our interviewees, because they find this process deeply meaningful.

8. How can the experience of meaning and meaningfulness be enhanced?

In addition to what impact can be owned by a philanthropist in their chosen domain and process, we think, carrying out deep reflections about the self has the potential to substantially enhance their experience of meaning and meaningfulness. At the most basic level, carrying out this reflection will help philanthropists recognise which object selves are exercising autonomy in their philanthropy; hence, they can prioritise them whenever possible when similar situations arise.

At a more complex level, carrying out this kind of reflection will help philanthropists' agentic self and meta-self gain clarity over what labels they should use to describe their object self, how they define these labels, and how they make sense of what should be prioritised, in which situation and why.

Often, this type of reflection cannot be confined just to the domain of philanthropy. It involves much deeper and broader reflections about their business self and personal self as well. Gaining the knowledge and skills to recognise a more comprehensive set of meaning sources that people can experience during their journey of creating philanthropic impact, we think, can hugely enhance the degree to which meaning and meaningfulness can be experienced in all aspects of their life.

9. What knowledge and skills can be acquired by HNWIs and UHNWIs to allow them to experience deeper meaning and more meaningful philanthropy?

Certainly, we believe that there are a distinct set of topics for self-reflection that would be helpful for HNWIs and UHNWIs. These have come up in our previous chapters, and they are different from the topics for self-reflection that might be used in other personal or business contexts.

Most of our interviewees have access to leadership advisors, business counsellors, philanthropic and financial advisors and leadership coaches, as well as a range of personal counselling services. Yet more than half of them shared that they have never been asked to reflect on their philanthropy and the role their own sense of self plays in its development – certainly not at the level of depth we enter into in this text. We think this is because none of these other professions have at their core the goal of stewarding the human capacity to love.

Understanding the relationships between different aspects of self, how these selves experience philanthropy, how they derive meaning and how this meaning contributes to feelings of self-worth and wellbeing as well as clarity over meaning in one's life is hugely important. This knowledge also allows people who are new to philanthropy to recognise that as they start their philanthropic journey, understanding the impact their philanthropy can make may be only part of the puzzle that they need to devote their attention to. It can be equally beneficial for them to reflect on why creating these impacts is so important for them personally. What does whether the impacts they set out to achieve can be achieved or not say about who the individual is or is beginning to become?

## A final thought

We began this study with the intent of studying philanthropists. As we conclude this summary of our research, we suggest that this identity label may be less than helpful. The identity of 'philanthropist' was rarely articulated by our interviewees and implies a generic whose existence we found little evidence for. Rather, a complex web of other individual or collective identities are typically in play. The most meaningful experiences our interviewees have are deeply expressive of self. Hence, who people are when they give (that is, their identity) seems to us to be hugely more powerful in shaping and sustaining giving than merely why people give. As a field and as a society, we have been fascinated by the latter. Work on motive abounds. The desire for impact, change or the need to make a difference are all commonly reported in sector surveys, but the focus is solely on the outcomes from philanthropy for the focal community. While this is understandable, in neglecting the former we fail to consider how giving can also impact the giver.

We believe that a failure to give sufficient weight to such impact is a mistake, because it can unnecessarily deprive individuals of meaning and, as a consequence, impact the sustainability of their engagement with philanthropy. Even if the goal is solely to support a focal community and the individual articulates their giving as entirely selfless, failure to consider how each experience might make the giver feel, can still hurt their sense of psychological wellbeing and lead to the early termination of support. Activities that lack meaning are quickly dropped. Time then for tired notions of altruism to be abandoned and replaced with an understanding of the journey in self that true engagement with philanthropy can create and the meaning it can deliver for all.

# References

Adler, J.M., Dunlop, W.L., Fivush, R., Lilgendahl, J.P., Lodi-Smith, J., McAdams, D.P., ... and Syed, M. (2017). Research methods for studying narrative identity: A primer. *Social Psychological and Personality Science*, 8(5), 519–527.

Andersen, S.M. and Chen, S. (2002). The relational self: An interpersonal social-cognitive theory. *Psychological Review*, 109(4), 619–645.

Aquino, K. and Reed, A., II (2002). The self-importance of moral identity. *Journal of Personality and Social Psychology*, 83(6), 1423–1440.

Arikan, A.M., Arikan, I. and Koparan, I. (2020). Creation opportunities: Entrepreneurial curiosity, generative cognition, and Knightian uncertainty. *Academy of Management Review*, 45(4), 808–824.

Aron, A., Aron, E.N. and Smollan, D. (1992). Inclusion of other in the Self Scale and the structure of interpersonal closeness. *Journal of Personality and Social Psychology*, 63(4), 596–612.

Bahl, S. and Milne, G.R. (2010). Talking to ourselves: A dialogical exploration of consumption experiences. *Journal of Consumer Research*, 37(1), 176–195.

Bailey, C., Yeoman, R., Madden, A., Thompson, M. and Kerridge, G. (2019). A review of the empirical literature on meaningful work: Progress and research agenda. *Human Resource Development Review*, 18(1), 83–113.

Bandura, A. (1977). Self-efficacy: Toward a unifying theory of behavioral change. *Psychological Review*, 84(2), 191–215.

Baumeister, R.F. (1991). *Meanings of Life*. New York: Guilford Press.

Baumeister, R.F. and Vohs, K.D. (2002). The pursuit of meaningfulness in life. In C.R. Snyder and S.J. Lopez (eds), *Handbook of Positive Psychology*. Oxford: Oxford University Press, pp 608–618.

Bekkers, R. and Wiepking, P. (2011). A literature review of empirical studies of philanthropy: Eight mechanisms that drive charitable giving. *Nonprofit and Voluntary Sector Quarterly*, 40(5), 924–973.

Belk, R.W. (1988). Possessions and the extended self. *Journal of Consumer Research*, 15(2), 139–168.

Boris, E.T. (1987). Creation and growth: A survey of private foundations. In T. Odendahl (ed), *America's Wealthy and the Future of Foundations*. New York: Foundation Center, pp 65–126.

Breeze, B. and Lloyd, T. (2013). *Richer Lives: Why Rich People Give*. London: Directory of Social Change.

Brooks, S. and Kumar, A. (2021). Why the super-rich will not be saving the world: Philanthropy and 'privatization creep' in global development. *Business & Society*, 62(2), 223–228.

Buchanan, P. (2019). *Giving Done Right: Effective Philanthropy and Making Every Dollar Count*. New York: Public Affairs.

Buss, D.M. and Craik, K.H. (1983). The act frequency approach to personality. *Psychological Review*, 90(2), 105–126.

Capgemini (2021). *World Wealth Report 2021*. Available at: https://worldwealthreport.com/ (accessed 8 January 2022).

Clark, M.S. and Mills, J. (1979). Interpersonal attraction in exchange and communal relationships. *Journal of Personality and Social Psychology*, 37(1), 12–24.

Collins, C. and Flannery, H. (2020). *Gilded Giving 2020: How Wealth Inequality Distorts Philanthropy and Imperils Democracy*. Institute for Policy Studies.

Coupe, T. and Monteiro, C. (2016). The charity of the extremely wealthy. *Economic Inquiry*, 54(2), 751–761.

Coutts (2017). *Coutts Million Dollar Donors Report 2017*. Available at: https://www.coutts.com/insight-articles/news/2017/million-pound-donors-report-2017.html (accessed 8 January 2022).

Dahling, J.J., Whitaker, B.G. and Levy, P.E. (2009). The development and validation of a new Machiavellianism scale. *Journal of Management*, 35(2), 219–257.

Dalzell, R.F. (2013). *The Good Rich and What They Cost Us: The Curious History of Wealth, Inequality, and American Democracy*. New Haven, CT: Yale University Press.

Davids, I. and Meijs, L. (2020). Can civil society be inclusive? Strategies for endowed foundations. *Learn Philanthropy Academy*, 12(4), 7–22.

Davidsson, P., Low, M.B. and Wright, M. (2001). Editor's introduction. Low and MacMillan ten years on: Achievements and future directions for entrepreneurship research. *Entrepreneurship Theory and Practice*, 25(4), 5–15.

Davis, M.H. (1983). Empathic concern and the muscular dystrophy telethon: Empathy as a multidimensional construct. *Personality and Social Psychology Bulletin*, 9(2), 223–229.

Deci, E.L. and Ryan, R.M. (1985). *Intrinsic Motivation and Self-Determination in Human Behavior*. New York: Plenum.

Dunlop, D.R. (1993). Major gift programs. In M.J. Worth (ed) *Educational Fund-Raising: Principles and Practice*. Pheonix, AZ: Oryx Press, pp 97–116.

Duquette, N.J. and Hargaden, E.P. (2021). Inequality and giving. *Journal of Economic Behavior & Organization*, 186, 189–200.

Eikenberry, A. and Mirabella, R.M. (2018). Extreme philanthropy: Philanthrocapitalism, effective altruism, and the discourse of neoliberalism. *PS: Political Science & Politics*, 51(1), 43–47.

Foy, S. and Gruber, M. (2022). Identity–society (mis)alignment and the instrumentalization of firm creation: Creative destruction and creative reconstruction. *Academy of Management Journal*, 65(2), 479–515.

Fredrickson, B.L. (2001). The role of positive emotions in positive psychology: The broaden-and-build theory of positive emotions. *American Psychologist*, 56(3), 218–226.

Frumkin, P. (2006). *Strategic Giving*. Chicago, IL: University of Chicago Press.

Gecas, V. (1991). The self-concept as a basis for a theory of motivation. In J.A. Howard and P.L. Callero (eds), *The Self-Society Dynamic: Cognition, Emotion, and Action*. New York: Cambridge University Press, pp 171–187.

Glaser, B.G. (1992). *Basics of Grounded Theory: Issues and Discussions*. Mill Valley, CA: Sociology Press.

Goetz, J.L., Keltner, D. and Simon-Thomas, E. (2010). Compassion: An evolutionary analysis and empirical review. *Psychological Bulletin*, 136(3), 351–374.

Grimes, M.G. (2018). The pivot: How founders respond to feedback through idea and identity work. *Academy of Management Journal*, 61(5), 1692–1717.

Haidt, J. (2001). The emotional dog and its rational tail: A social intuitionist approach to moral judgment. *Psychological Review*, 108(4), 814–834.

Hart, D., Atkins, R. and Ford, D. (1998). Urban America as a context for the development of moral identity in adolescence. *Journal of Social Issues*, 54(3), 513–530.

Havens, J.J., O'Herlihy, M.A. and Schervish, P.G. (2006). Charitable giving: How much, by whom, to what, and how. In W.W. Powell and R. Steinberg (eds), *The Nonprofit Sector: A Research Handbook* (2nd ed). New Haven, CT: Yale Press, pp 542–567.

Heine, S.J., Proulx, T. and Vohs, K.D. (2006). The meaning maintenance model: On the coherence of social motivations. *Personality and Social Psychology Review*, 10(2), 88–110.

Heintzelman, S.J. and King, L.A. (2014). Life is pretty meaningful. *American Psychologist*, 69(6), 561–574.

Hermans, H.J., Kempen, H.J. and Van Loon, R.J. (1992). The dialogical self: Beyond individualism and rationalism. *American Psychologist*, 47(1), 23–33.

Herzog, P.S. and Price, H.E. (2016). *American Generosity: Who Gives and Why*. Oxford: Oxford University Press.

Hickman, K., Shrader, M., Xu, D. and Lawson, D. (2015). The Forbes 400 and the Gates-Buffett giving pledge. *ACRN Journal of Finance and Risk Perspectives*, 4(1), 82–101.

Hicks, J.A., Schlegel, R.J. and King, L.A. (2010). Social threats, happiness, and the dynamics of meaning in life judgments. *Personality and Social Psychology Bulletin*, 36(10), 1305–1317.

Kilby, P. (1971). *Entrepreneurship and Economic Development*. New York: Free Press.

Kim, J., Chen, K., Rivera, G.N., Hong, E.K., Kamble, S., Scollon, C.N., … and Schlegel, R.J. (2022). True-self-as-guide lay theory endorsement across five countries. *Self and Identity*, 21(8), 939–962.

King, L.A. and Hicks, J.A. (2021). The science of meaning in life. *Annual Review of Psychology*, 72, 561–584.

Legrand, D. and Ruby, P. (2009). What is self-specific? Theoretical investigation and critical review of neuroimaging results. *Psychological Review*, 116(1), 252–282.

Locke, K. (2001). *Grounded Theory in Management Research.* London: Sage.

Locke, K., Feldman, M. and Golden-Biddle, K. (2022). Coding practices and iterativity: Beyond templates for analyzing qualitative data. *Organizational Research Methods*, 25(2), 262–284.

Lumpkin, G.T. and Dess, G.G. (1996). Clarifying the entrepreneurial orientation construct and linking it to performance. *Academy of Management Review*, 21(1), 135–172.

Lysova, E.I., Allan, B.A., Dik, B.J., Duffy, R.D. and Steger, M.F. (2019). Fostering meaningful work in organizations: A multi-level review and integration. *Journal of Vocational Behavior*, 110, 374–389.

MacAskill, W. (2016). *Doing Good Better: Effective Altruism and a Radical New Way to Make a Difference.* New York: Avery.

Maclean, M., Harvey, C., Gordon, J. and Shaw, E. (2015). Identity, storytelling and the philanthropic journey. *Human Relations*, 68(10), 1623–1652.

Madden, A. and Bailey, C. (2019). Self-transcendence and meaningful work. In R. Yeoman, C. Bailey, A. Madden and M. Thompson (eds), *The Oxford Handbook of Meaningful Work.* Oxford: Oxford University Press, pp 148–164.

Markus, H. and Wurf, E. (1987). The dynamic self-concept: A social psychological perspective. *Annual Review of Psychology*, 38, 299–337.

Markus, H.R. and Kitayama, S. (1991). Culture and the self: Implications for cognition, emotion, and motivation. *Psychological Review*, 98(2), 224–253.

Martela, F. and Steger, M.F. (2016). The three meanings of meaning in life: Distinguishing coherence, purpose, and significance. *The Journal of Positive Psychology*, 11(5), 531–545.

Maslow, A.H. (1968). *Toward a Psychology of Being* (2nd ed). New York: Van Nostrand Reinhold.

McAdams, D.P. (2011). Narrative identity. In S.J. Schwartz, K. Luyckx and V.L. Vignoles (eds), *Handbook of Identity Theory and Research.* New York: Springer, pp 99–115.

McBride, R. (2022). Deontic binding: Imposed, voluntary, and autogenic. *Social Epistemology*, 36(2), 218–237.

# References

McBride, R. and Wuebker, R. (2022). Social objectivity and entrepreneurial opportunities. *Academy of Management Review*, 47(1), 75–92.

Meer, J. and Priday, B.A. (2021). Generosity across the income and wealth distributions. *National Tax Journal*, 74(3), 655–687.

Mischel, W. and Shoda, Y. (1995). A cognitive-affective system theory of personality: Reconceptualizing situations, dispositions, dynamics, and invariance in personality structure. *Psychological Review*, 102(2), 246–268.

Neumayr, M. and Pennerstorfer, A. (2021). The relation between income and donations as a proportion of income revisited: Literature review and empirical application. *Nonprofit and Voluntary Sector Quarterly*, 50(3), 551–577.

Newman, G.E., Bloom, P. and Knobe, J. (2014). Value judgments and the true self. *Personality and Social Psychology Bulletin*, 40(2), 203–216.

Nielsen, W.A. (1985). *The Golden Donors*. New York: Truman-Talley.

Osili, U. (2011). *Review of Literature on Giving and High Net Worth Individuals*. Indianapolis: The Center on Philanthropy at Indiana University. Available at: https://scholarworks.iupui.edu/server/api/core/bitstreams/e6538a57-3b9f-4450-ae40-f11729aa8304/content (accessed 2 March 2022).

Osili, U.O., Ackerman, J. and Li, Y. (2019). Economic effects on million dollar giving. *Nonprofit and Voluntary Sector Quarterly*, 48(2), 417–439.

Osili, U., Clark, C. and Bergdoll, J. (2021). *The 2021 Bank of America Study of Philanthropy: Charitable Giving by Affluent Households*. Indianapolis: Indiana University Lilly Family School of Philanthropy.

Ostrower, F. (1995). *Why the Wealthy Give: The Culture of Elite Philanthropy*. Princeton, NJ: Princeton University Press.

Oveis, C., Horberg, E.J. and Keltner, D. (2010). Compassion, pride, and social intuitions of self-other similarity. *Journal of Personality and Social Psychology*, 98(4), 618–630.

Pierce, J.L., Kostova, T. and Dirks, K.T. (2001). Toward a theory of psychological ownership in organizations. *Academy of Management Review*, 26(2), 298–310.

Pratt, M.G. and Ashforth, B.E. (2003). Fostering meaningfulness in working and at work. In K.S. Cameron, J.E. Dutton and R.E. Quinn (eds), *Positive Organizational Scholarship*. San Francisco, CA: Berrett-Koehler Publishers Inc, pp 309–327.

Prince, R.A. and File, K.M. (1994). *The Seven Faces of Philanthropy*. San Francisco, CA: Wiley.

Reed, A., II and Forehand, M. (2019). *Handbook of Research on Identity Theory in Marketing*. Cheltenham: Edward Elgar Publishing.

Reich, R. (2020). *Just Giving: Why Philanthropy Is Failing Democracy and How It Can Do Better*. Princeton, NJ: Princeton University Press.

Rosso, B.D., Dekas, K.H. and Wrzesniewski, A. (2010). On the meaning of work: A theoretical integration and review. *Research in Organizational Behavior*, 30, 91–127.

Sargeant, A. and Lee, S. (2002). Individual and contextual antecedents of donor trust in the voluntary sector. *Journal of Marketing Management*, 18(7–8), 779–802.

Sargeant, A. and Shang, J. (2010). *Fundraising: Principles and Practice*. San Francisco, CA: Jossey-Bass.

Sargeant, A. and Shang, J. (2016). Risk perception and management in development philanthropy. *Voluntary Sector Review*, 7(3), 251–267.

Sargeant, A. and Shang, J. (2017). *Fundraising Principles and Practice* (2nd ed). Hoboken NY: John Wiley and Sons.

Schervish, P.G. (2006). The moral biography of wealth: Philosophical reflections on the foundation of philanthropy. *Nonprofit and Voluntary Sector Quarterly*, 35(3), 477–492.

Schervish, P.G. (2007). Why the wealthy give. In M. Moody and B. Breeze (eds), *The Philanthropy Reader*. Abingdon: Routledge, pp 195–200.

Schervish, P.G. (2008). Why the wealthy give: Factors which mobilize philanthropy among high net-worth individuals. In A. Sargeant and W. Wymer, Jr (eds), *The Routledge Companion to Nonprofit Marketing*, New York: Routledge, pp 165–181.

Schervish, P.G. (2009). Beyond self-interest and altruism: Care as mutual nourishment. *Conversations on Philanthropy: Emerging Questions on Liberality and Social Thought*, VI. Available at: www.conversationsonphilanthropy.org/journal-contribution/beyond-self-interest-and-altruism-care-as-mutual-nourishment/ (accessed 8 January 2022).

Schervish, P.G. and Herman, A. (1988). *Empowerment and Beneficence: Strategies of Living and Giving among the Wealthy*. Chestnut Hill, MA: Social Welfare Regional Research Institute, Boston College. Available at: www.bc.edu/content/dam/files/research_sites/cwp/pdf/empandben.pdf (accessed 8 January 2022).

Schervish, P.G. and Havens. J.J. (2002). The new physics of philanthropy: The supply side vectors of charitable giving: Part II: The spiritual side of the supply side. *CASE International Journal of Educational Advancement*, 2(3), 221–241.

Schervish, P.G. and Whitaker, K. (2010). *Wealth and the Will of God*. Bloomington: Indiana University Press.

Schervish, P.G., O'Herlihy, M.A. and Havens. J.J. (2001). *Agent Animated Wealth and Philanthropy: The Dynamics of Accumulation and Allocation among High-Tech Donors*. Chestnut Hill, MA: Social Welfare Research Institute, Boston College. Available at: https://dlib.bc.edu/islandora/object/bc-ir:104104/datastream/PDF/view (accessed 8 January 2022).

Schervish, P.G., Coutsoukis, P.E. and Lewis, E. (2005). *Gospels of Wealth: How the Rich Portray their Lives*. Praeger: London.

Schlegel, R.J., Hicks, J.A., Davis, W.E., Hirsch, K.A. and Smith, C.M. (2013). The dynamic interplay between perceived true self-knowledge and decision satisfaction. *Journal of Personality and Social Psychology*, 104(3), 542–558.

Schumpeter, J.A. (1935). The analysis of economic change. *The Review of Economics and Statistics*, 17(4), 2–10.

Sellen, C. (2021). Philanthropy as a self-taxation mechanism with happy outcomes: Crafting a new public discourse. In H. Peter and G. Lideikyte Huber (eds), *The Routledge Handbook of Taxation and Philanthropy*. New York: Routledge, pp 298–324.

Shang, J. (2019). Identity and charitable giving: The six-self framework. In A. Reed II and M. Forehand (eds), *Handbook of Research on Identity Theory in Marketing*. Cheltenham: Edward Elgar, pp 417–433.

Sheldon, K.M. and Elliott, A.J. (1998). Goal striving, need satisfaction and longitudinal well-being: The self-concordance model. *Journal of Personality and Social Psychology*, 76(3), 482–497.

Sheldon, K.M., Ryan, R.M., Rawsthorne, L.J. and Ilardi, B. (1997). Trait self and true self: Cross-role variation in the Big-Five personality traits and its relations with psychological authenticity and subjective well-being. *Journal of Personality and Social Psychology*, 73(6), 1380–1393.

Shepherd, D.A., Wennberg, K., Suddaby, R. and Wiklund, J. (2019). What are we explaining? A review and agenda on initiating, engaging, performing, and contextualizing entrepreneurship. *Journal of Management*, 45(1), 159–196.

Skitka, L.J. and Mullen, E. (2002). The dark side of moral conviction. *Analyses of Social Issues and Public Policy*, 2(1), 35–41.

Skitka, L.J., Hanson, B.E., Morgan, G.S. and Wisneski, D.C. (2021). The psychology of moral conviction. *Annual Review of Psychology*, 72, 347–366.

Spectrum Group (2021). New Spectrum study reveals US household wealth climbed to record levels in 2020 after rebounding from the March pandemic-related market crash. Available at: https://spectrum.com/Content_Press/spectrem-press-release-march-15-2021.aspx (accessed 8 January 2022).

Spreitzer, G., Sutcliffe, K., Dutton, J., Sonenshein, S. and Grant, A.M. (2005). A socially embedded model of thriving at work. *Organization Science*, 16(5), 537–549.

Sternberg, R.J. (1986). A triangular theory of love. *Psychological Review*, 93(2), 119–135.

Stevenson, H. and Jarillo, J.C. (1990). A paradigm of entrepreneurship: Entrepreneurial management, *Strategic Management Journal*, 11, 17–27.

Strathman, A., Gleicher, F., Boninger, D.S. and Edwards, C.S. (1994). The consideration of future consequences: Weighing immediate and distant outcomes of behavior. *Journal of Personality and Social Psychology*, 66(4), 742–752.

Strauss, A.L. and Corbin, J. (1998). *Basics of Qualitative Research: Techniques and Procedures for Developing Grounded Theory* (2nd ed). Thousand Oaks, CA: Sage.

Strohminger, N., Knobe, J. and Newman, G. (2017). The true self: A psychological concept distinct from the self. *Perspectives on Psychological Science*, 12(4), 551–560.

Sulek, M. (2010). On the modern meaning of philanthropy. *Nonprofit and Voluntary Sector Quarterly*, 39(2), 193–212.

Swann, W.B., Jr, Jetten, J., Gómez, Á., Whitehouse, H. and Bastian, B. (2012). When group membership gets personal: A theory of identity fusion. *Psychological Review*, 119(3), 441–456.

Tajfel, H. and Turner, J.C. (2004). An integrative theory of intergroup conflict. In M.J. Hatch and M. Schultz (eds), *Organizational Identity: A Reader*. Oxford: Oxford University Press, pp 56–65.

Tangney, J.P., Baumeister, R.F. and Boone, A.L. (2004). High self-control predicts good adjustment, less pathology, better grades, and interpersonal success. *Journal of Personality*, 72(2), 271–324.

Vohs, K.D., Aaker, J.L. and Catapano, R. (2019). It's not going to be that fun: Negative experiences can add meaning to life. *Current Opinion in Psychology*, 26, 11–14.

Walker, L.J. and Frimer, J.A. (2007). Moral personality of brave and caring exemplars. *Journal of Personality and Social Psychology*, 93(5), 845–860.

Washburn, E. (2023). What to know about effective altruism—championed by Musk, Bankman-Fried and Silicon Valley giants. *Forbes*, 8 March. Available at: www.forbes.com/sites/emilywashburn/2023/03/08/what-to-know-about-effective-altruism-championed-by-musk-bankman-fried-and-silicon-valley-giants/?sh=69f6355e2362 (accessed 19 February 2024).

Weiss, J.W., Skelley, M.F., Haughey, J.C. and Hall, D.T. (2004). Calling, new careers and spirituality: A reflective perspective for organizational leaders and professionals. In M.L. Pava and P. Primeaux (eds), *Spiritual Intelligence at Work: Meaning, Metaphor and Morals*. Amsterdam: Elsevier, pp 175–201.

Wiepking, P. and Bekkers, R. (2012). Who gives? A literature review of predictors of charitable giving. Part two: Gender, family composition and income. *Voluntary Sector Review*, 3(2), 217–245.

Winton, B.G., Whittington, J.L. and Meskelis, S. (2022). Authentic leadership: Making meaning and building engagement. *European Business Review*, 34(5), 689–705.

Worth, M.J., Pandey, S., Pandey, S.K. and Qadummi, S. (2019). Understanding motivations of mega-gift donors to higher education: A qualitative study. *Public Administration Review*, 80(2), 281–293.

# Index

Made in the USA
Middletown, DE
10 August 2024